SURVIVING
SUICIDAL
IDEATION

Surviving Suicidal Ideation

From Therapy to Spirituality and the Lived Experience

Authored By Gina Cavalier & Dr. Amelia Kelley

Original Art By Gina Cavalier

SWEDENBORG FOUNDATION
Royersford, Pennsylvania

Throughout this work, citations to Emanuel Swedenborg's works refer to Swedenborg's section numbers, which are uniform in all editions, rather than page numbers.

All hand-drawn illustrations in this book are the work and copyright of Gina Cavalier, used with permission.

No part of this book was created by artificial intelligence.

Limit of Liability/Disclaimer of Warranty: The publisher and the authors are providing this book and its contents on an "as is" basis and make no representations or warranties of any kind with respect to this book or its contents. No warranty may be created or extended by sales or promotional materials. The publisher and the authors disclaim all such representations and warranties, including but not limited to warranties of healthcare and/or fitness for a particular purpose. In addition, the publisher and the authors assume no responsibility for errors, inaccuracies, omissions, or any other inconsistencies herein. Neither the publisher nor the authors shall be liable for damages arising herefrom. The fact that an individual, organization or website is referred to in this work as a citation and/or potential source of further information does not mean that the authors or the publisher endorse the information the individual, organization or website may provide or recommendations they may make.

This work is sold with the understanding that the publisher is not engaged in rendering medical, legal, or other professional advice or services. The content of this book is for informational purposes only and is not intended to diagnose, treat, cure, or prevent any condition or disease, nor is it meant as a substitute for direct expert assistance. The advice and strategies contained herein may not be suitable for every situation. If assistance is required, the services of a competent professional should be sought.

Library of Congress Cataloging-in-Publication Data

Names: Cavalier, Gina M., author. | Kelley, Amelia, author.
Title: Surviving suicidal ideation : from therapy to spirituality and the
   lived experience / Gina Cavalier and Dr. Amelia Kelley.

Description: Royersford, Pennsylvania : Swedenborg Foundation, [2024] |
   Includes bibliographical references.

Identifiers: LCCN 2023052045 | ISBN 9780877853657 (paperback) | ISBN
   9780877857334 (epub)
Subjects: LCSH: Suicide. | Suicide--Prevention. | BISAC: PSYCHOLOGY /
   Suicide | SELF-HELP / Spiritual

Classification: LCC HV6545 .C266 2024 | DDC 362.28--dc23/eng/20240422

LC record available at https://lccn.loc.gov/2023052045

Printed in the United States of America

Cover illustration by Gina Cavalier

Design by Karen Connor

Swedenborg Foundation
70 Buckwalter Road
Suite 900 PMB 405
Royersford, PA 19468
www.swedenborg.com

Contents

List of Journal Prompts

List of Exercises

List of Meditations

Notes from the Authors

DUE TO THE sensitive nature of the overall topic, only you know where you are at any given time, so please use your discretion if anything is triggering and move away from that topic or portion of the material. Some might want to go through the book linearly, and others might choose to pick the topics and exercises that feel right for them at the time. We have included a personalized safety plan on page 71 to support your journey; this could be a great first step in your exploration.

Parts of this work are from one of the author's personal lived experiences with suicidal ideation and her personal research into seeking healing therapies, practitioners, and modalities to help stop and manage her suicidal thoughts. Her opinions, expressions, or experiences may not be good suggestions for the general public or for someone dealing with a specific diagnosis.

This book is written with the best intentions to support those suffering either with the thoughts of suicide or someone who is living with grief from the death of a loved who died by suicide. The thoughts and opinions thereafter might speak to the reader, or they might not. If any portions do not resonate, we suggest you take what works for you and leave the rest.

The nature of suicide makes getting concrete data and statistics difficult, and it changes constantly. Most of the information provided is from research done in 2023.

The Artwork by Gina

ART IS MY soul's way of helping me process anxious energy and past trauma. But I didn't always know this about my doodles. The "aha" came when I was in my mid-thirties. I was in Philadelphia working on a project with Joe Frazier, the boxer, for a friend of mine with HBO. I was hired to follow Frazier around and take pictures of him living his busy life.

It was a very intense week, and I felt completely overwhelmed by the energy and all the moving parts. At the same time, Frazier was such a fascinating person that I wanted to capture the memories of this moment mentally. One night at dinner with a fully seated crowd at the table, I sat next to Joe. My brain felt like it was breaking, and I needed a reprieve but didn't feel like I could leave. So, I did what I always do in these situations. I took the napkins on the table and I started to draw and close out the energies around me like a giant wall. Joe looked at my friend and asked, "Why is she doing that?" My friend said, "She does this whenever she gets overwhelmed. She turns her pain and anxiety into art." It was the first time I had heard it described this way, and I needed to hear it. It stuck, and soon after, I shifted my perspective when I said out loud, "I'm an artist!" I had reserved that title for other people who, I felt, had superior art, talent, or education. I would get anxious and excited in the art store like a kid in the candy store. My mind would toggle between "Do you belong here? You are just a doodler," and affirming my stake in this world as a true artist. I was afraid at first of making a mess of the art paper until I told myself that it was okay to make a mess. It just means that I'm creating new standards for myself every day, and that is a good thing.

I now understand art as an inborn, intuitive pathway for me to release trauma and anxiety. I feel so connected to the world around me when I draw and am grateful to have images that represent many parts of me while bringing in others to gaze upon them.

Foreword by Thomas Moore

ONE DAY THE phone rang, and a client told me nervously that she had a knife in her hand and a rope around her neck. I truly love most of my therapy clients, maybe all of them, and the last thing I want any of them to do is end their lives. But I don't think it helps for me to become hysterical and consumed with my need to stop them from killing themselves.

So within seconds of this call, I relaxed and talked to the woman calmly, focusing on her need to present me with a drama apparently intended to express something important. I am always worried about a strong fantasy slipping into acting-out, but my worry isn't going to help as much as close attention to her words and actions.

Anyone can reach a point where life is so difficult and discouraging that you have thoughts of ending it all. This doesn't mean that you are crazy or mentally ill or a failure. The thoughts come. True, they may indicate the seriousness of your despair, but you don't create them. Quite naturally, they accompany disheartening moments in life, or they may reveal hidden developments that haven't fully come to light. They even make sense. You are doing your best, but life feels impossible, and you don't see any alternatives for something remotely like a solution.

The trouble with suicidal thoughts is that you might possibly act on them, make them literal. That is a tragedy for you and for anyone who loves you. But you might act out other less-dire feelings, as well. You may be having trouble maintaining a peaceful relationship with your life partner. One day you "lose it" and say things you shouldn't. You may end up divorced, which is a tragedy, too, perhaps. Only, it isn't the end of your life.

My point is that acting out a state of mind is often the real problem. Whenever I hear that someone I know or know of has committed suicide, I feel sad, wishing we could have talked it through. I don't think I have any magic power to help a person hold back from killing himself, but I know the difference between feeling that you have no options and ending your life. There is always more to talk through.

As a therapist, I have had clients who get into a place where thoughts of suicide float around them like constant companions. There seems to be something attractive and satisfying in them. These thoughts give pleasure in an odd sort of way. I want to be careful not to react to these thoughts hysterically or to rush into savior or hero mode. I want to take them seriously, explore them, and listen to what they are trying to say.

> **Some kind of self may need to die so that another more successful one can live. It can be confusing whether I should end my way of life or my life itself.**

If you take these thoughts literally, you will want to banish them, but if you understand them in a layered fashion, where deeper meanings lie beneath the surface, you may catch their poetic resonance. "I want to kill myself" could mean, "I want to get rid of the particular self that has caused me pain." "I want to end my life" may mean, "I don't want this disaster of a life any longer."

Maybe the current approach to life or the sense of self needs to end. Not literal life but the story being lived may not support a meaningful and tolerable life. Some kind of self may need to die so that another more successful one can live. It can be confusing whether I should end my way of life or my life itself.

When my old friend and colleague James Hillman was just beginning his productive career, he wrote the book *Suicide and the Soul*.[1] His main idea was that thoughts of suicide speak to the soul and not entirely to the surface of life. Deep in the soul, something may very well need to die, perhaps so that there may be new life, a profound transformation. For aid, you need someone nearby who understands the layered meaning of death and is not distracted by their need to prevent acting out.

Psychotherapists are trained to know the difference between their own feelings and those of their clients. But the ordinary person, not so trained, may confuse their fears with those of their friends. A person who wants to help may be afraid of thoughts of ending it, and their efforts on behalf of a friend may in part be a way of protecting themselves from the horror of suicide. You have to know yourself quite well if you want to help a suicidal friend stay safe.

I often say that anyone can have a "therapist within," not inappropriately playing at being the therapist but more honestly and deeply knowing that they have a natural aptitude for helping people. Such gifted people who want to help a person deal with suicidal thoughts could read up on the basics of good therapeutic technique and bring more awareness to the task of helping others. It isn't rocket science, but it is a subtle business that requires intelligence and skill.

When I published my most popular book, *Care of the Soul*,[2] the very first line said it all: "The great malady of this century, implicated in all of our troubles and affecting us individually and socially, is 'loss of soul.'" For millennia, the greatest teachers have said that the soul is the source of life. It is our essence and the root of our being. They also warn that we have to care for this soul, or it can be wounded or can even vanish.

1. James Hillman, *Suicide and the Soul,* 1973.
2. Thomas Moore, *Care of the Soul, Twenty-fifth Anniversary Ed: A Guide for Cultivating Depth and Sacredness in Everyday Life,* Harper Perennial, New York, 2016.

How do you care for your soul? By making a good home for yourself suitable for your life situation. By eating healthy food and dining in a pleasurable way with friends and family. By having a good connection with the natural world, if only by having a parakeet or a bonsai tree in your home. By developing intimacy with a friend, lover, or neighbor. By having a vision for your future and your place on the planet. By having deep and meaningful conversations on a regular basis.

When your soul is cared for, you will feel deep, inner security and purpose. You won't be enticed to end your life but will find a way to survive because the soul urges toward life. Marsilio Ficino, the Renaissance philosopher and magus who has been the focus of much of my scholarly research, said that the soul exists in both time and eternity.[3] There is something timeless in ourselves, in our soul, that is not affected by the twists and turns of life experience. It is as though a shield around the soul keeps it safe from timebound realities.

The timeless soul may help avoid the temptation of suicide, and that implies some sort of spiritual discussion. You may need an expanded vision, a bigger outlook, and a source of realistic, hard-won hope. If you don't have an expansive, perhaps spiritual, outlook, the despair housed in your small world can suffocate you. Almost any kind of genuine spiritual practice can help by giving you a crack in your limited world, a way out of it into real possibility.

Living more from the deep soul than from superficial purposes and understandings may keep you closer to life and, therefore, perhaps less prone to dispense with life through suicide. Thoughts of suicide arise more from weakness than strength and from a weak understanding of what is going on and how life works. But the soul offers deep inner power and is equal to the luring temptations of suicide.

This book is a rich resource for people dealing with thoughts of suicide. For me, the best part is Gina's moving story of dead-ends

3. Josephine L. Burroughs, "Marsilio Ficino, Platonic Theology," *Journal of the History of Ideas* (1944): 227–242.

and discoveries. Going through many different trials and challenges, a good story is usually better than advice and recommendations. You find inspiring narratives in ancient myths and fairy tales where the main character has to find a way through seemingly impossible ordeals. If the story is true to life and ancient, it comes from deep in the human soul. Gina's story is heartfelt, open, and complicated. She tells it in a way that you feel her passions and her disappointments. In the end, you are relieved that she found her way back into life.

I suggest reading Gina's story more than once to notice the subtle details that can offer you guidance. Don't feel alone. Your path has been walked before, and the seasoned survivors know a thing or two about it. Her narrative may help you sort out your own and may help you find ways to alter it toward hope.

This book also offers you a treasury of resources, for there is a secret about human life not often presented in stark terms: to get through life's toughest and complicated challenges, we need each other. I'm a professional psychotherapist, and yet deep down, I am basically one human being accompanying another as they find their way through the maze of human problems. You can do it professionally or personally. This book offers you both: professional resources in the margins and a beautiful, exemplary story in the center.

This book is also the work of Dr. Amelia Kelley, an accomplished therapist who has a wide range of skills and expertise. I live with a former yoga instructor and art therapist, now a full-time painter, so I appreciate Dr. Kelley's contributions in a personal way. I have spent my life shaping an approach to therapy that includes spirituality and art, and I often say to therapists I am teaching that whether or not they know it, they are spiritual directors, as well. Every human being is made of body, soul, and spirit and needs guidance in all areas. Dr. Kelley knows the experience of trauma from many sides, giving this book the substance and edge of understanding needed in the world. I am terribly impressed by her educational background, her work experience, and her fortitude for getting out in public and making a difference.

Introduction

THIS BOOK IS written for your survival. The topics covered and stories told may be difficult to read, but we are confident that with self-compassion and the skills provided, you will learn to thrive and connect with your reason to live.

The stories told come from a lived experience of survival, as one of the coauthors, Gina Cavalier, herself suffered years of suicidal thoughts and ideation, but she is here now, dedicating herself to you. Directed by her soul and spirit guides, this book unfolds as a case study of how she was able to overcome her own suicidality. She has committed to sharing her past experiences openly and honestly, led by the desire to relate and connect with other survivors. As you learn of Gina's experiences, Dr. Amelia Kelley will provide research-supported strategies for how to overcome these and similar experiences, while providing the framework for the **5 Phases of Suicidal Ideation,** which you will learn to identify and work through. The phases are **Phase 1: Contemplation, Phase 2: Hopelessness, Phase 3: Despair, Phase 4: Intent, and Phase 5: Action.** When experiencing thoughts of suicide, it is normal to shift between phases rapidly; in the pages of this book, we will teach you how to navigate and cope with these experiences.

 When hearing from Gina, you will see a circle with her initials at the beginning of the section.

(ak) When hearing from Amelia, a circle with her initials will appear.

In this book you will learn the same therapeutic tools that helped save Gina's own life, while being grounded by life-guiding principles taught by philosopher and theologian Emanuel Swedenborg, whose life mission was to share spiritually uplifting literature with the world. When considering how we, the authors, wanted to reach those suffering from suicidal ideation, we were confident that the Swedenborg Foundation could truly support our mission to save the lives of our readers.

Emanuel Swedenborg was a scientist and Swedish nobleman who lived in the eighteenth century in Stockholm, Sweden. He underwent a spiritual awakening in his mid-fifties that opened his spiritual eyes to the realities of realms beyond the material world, a perception that was continuous and remained for the duration of his physical lifetime. He published eighteen titles detailing his spiritual experiences and what he learned through them, including the nature of spiritual language, the qualities of spirits, angels, and demons, and how our soul lives in and through our body.

In addition to Dr. Amelia Kelley's grasp of the evidence-based therapeutic modalities to support healing and Gina Cavalier's firsthand experience of surviving suicidality and connecting to her wholeness, Emanuel Swedenborg will be your third guide in this journey. You will find insights quoted from his works interspersed throughout the text from his years spent studying the nature of life after death and our direct connection to it within.

Altogether, it is our sincere wish that this triad of support serves you in your healing journey as you recover wounded parts of yourself and reconnect to your wholeness and the eternal resources of love and wisdom within your own consciousness.

If you are feeling sad and alone or have lost a sense of hope, we beg you to hold on, even if it's for one more day, to get the help and support you deserve. Simply picking this book up is an act of courage and shows that a great part of you wants to live. In the second part of the book, you will learn about the **5 Phases of Healing from**

Suicidality, namely **Phase 1: Realization; Phase 2: Clarity; Phase 3: Motivation; Phase 4: Resilience;** and **Phase 5: Confidence.**

As you work through the book, we want to support your journey and encourage you to reach out to either author with any questions you may have. You can find Gina Cavalier at theliberatedhealer.com and Dr. Amelia Kelley at ameliakelley.com. However, if at any point while reading you feel you are in crisis, we urge you to seek help immediately. You can find resources to do so in the appendix of this book (on page 212), which includes a comprehensive list of crisis lifelines and suicide prevention and information and resources.

We also feel it necessary to highlight the gravity of this subject and that this book is not intended to replace mental health services, medical interventions, or prescriptions necessary to keep those experiencing suicidal ideation safe and alive. We encourage you instead to think of this book as a companion to support your journey of healing and as a way to fortify your desire to live. Know that every word was written with unconditional love and gratitude for the opportunity to work alongside you. We hope you will feel connected with a sense of peace and find your reasons for moving forward, fully alive. 🖤

SURVIVING SUICIDAL IDEATION

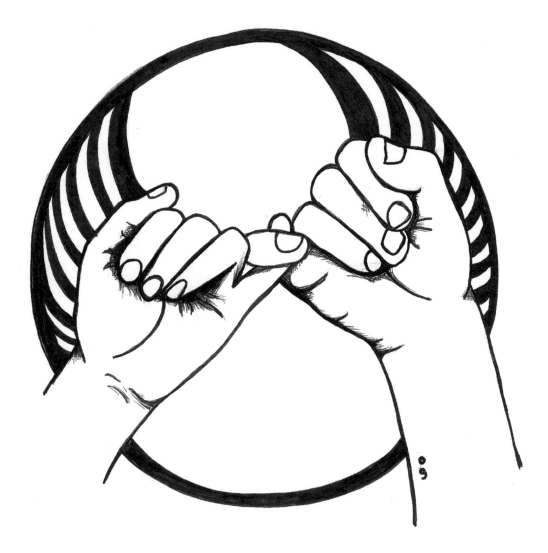

PART 1
The What of Suicidal Ideation
Chapter 1: The Essentials

There is a spiritual world and a natural world within each of us. The deeper elements, which belong to our minds and relate to our intellect and will, constitute our spiritual world, while the outer elements, which belong to our bodies and relate to our senses and actions, constitute our natural world. —Emanuel Swedenborg, Heaven and Hell 90

UNDERSTANDING SUICIDE IS no easy task. The Centers for Disease Control reported it being the 11th leading cause of death in the United States in recent years.[4] It can be difficult to discuss and has remained a taboo subject in many ways. The reasons behind suicidal thoughts vary from unshakable feelings of despair, grief, and loneliness to mental health issues, poverty, and a lack of open dialogue about prevention. This is why suicide should be at the forefront of conversations and something discussed without shame, reserve, or secrecy.

Many of us struggle when there are no definitive answers to solve suffering, and the answer here is not black or white. That is why in this book we are calling for a monumental shift in how we *think* about suicide. We need to unlearn the misperceptions that further perpetuate unhelpful ways of trying to solve such a complex issue. Instead of simply looking at how to prevent the act of suicide itself, we want to help you find reasons not to commit suicide and to live fully in the first place. To provide this, you will find compassionate,

4. "Suicide and Self-Harm Injury," Centers for Disease Control and Prevention, accessed April 9, 2024, https://.cdc.gov/nchs/fastats/suicide.htm.

holistic, spiritually driven approaches to recovering from suicidality with the ultimate goal of keeping you alive. ☙

gc A CHILD'S HEART HURTS

As I recall, my suicidal thoughts began at around eight or nine, when my biological parents split up. I wasn't upset due to their separation; even as a child, it was obvious they needed to be away from each other. But I was old enough to feel the heavy toxicity surrounding my life with no safety net in sight. Both of my parents came from abusive and neglectful families, and they were continuing what they were taught, leaving me feeling, fearful, lonely, and disconnected.

With fresh eyes looking at the world, a child's heart will find beauty even if atrocities surround them. I had hope that things would get better, and I did my part to try and bring happiness to everyone around me. Yet, I felt displaced and forgotten. I carried that feeling deep within me until I progressed through the **5 Phases of Healing** detailed in Chapter 4 and **Forgiveness** in Chapter 7.

I was a sickly child with black circles around my eyes and was underweight (landing me the nickname "Spaghetti Legs"), with a steady stream of fevers. It was believed I suffered from chronic Valley Fever, a common ailment amongst our community in Scottsdale, Arizona. My parents couldn't afford medical care, and I would stay sick for long periods with painful earaches and allergy symptoms. To treat me, they would stick me in ice baths to eliminate the fevers. I loathed the ice, which felt like a punishment for being sick. The proudest part of my childhood was being the sidekick to my brother, Johnny, who was five years older than me. He would watch out for and protect me. He was a light, funny, kind soul, and I looked up to him.

It was the '70s, and post-war flower power was in full effect, making drinking and smoking in large quantities acceptable. My parents embraced this newfound social freedom. When my father drank, he would take it to the extreme and almost always blacked out, violently beating anything around him. He was a binge drinker, and when he started to drink, it would last weeks or months until he decided he needed a break. Those chapters of my life were frightening because nobody knew who or what would be the target of his anger. Nights were sleepless and full of fear. The holidays were the worst, as they always brought a reason to celebrate with alcohol. I have many memories of my mother, brother, and me running to the car to get away from my father, driving all night to our nearest relatives' home in Southern California. My mother would fight back as much as she could, even though she was only 5 feet tall and 95 pounds. I watched her one night, with marks all over her as she jumped inside his truck. Without a second thought, she revved the engine and drove it into the kitchen wall, which she managed to ram in roughly 3 feet. To this day, I don't know if she was trying to kill herself, or my father, or if it was an accident, but dramatic shows of her frustration were a normal occurrence for my mother. Seeing the neighbors coming out of their homes with folded arms was always an embarrassment. I would look at them and ask myself, "Can I come live with you? Why didn't I get a loving family like yours?"

When you are young, it's hard to understand how the cards of life could be handed out like this. I began to pity myself, another thing I carried into adulthood. This also put me in danger because I would seek attention from literally anyone else, and that longing made me feel even more unwanted and unworthy when unrequited. I likened it to being a wolf shunned from the pack or a bird pushed out of the nest. You are defective and don't belong.

Eventually, my father met his next female conquest. I innocently asked my mother, "Why was Dad in a lady's house in his underwear?" I had seen him in the neighbor's house with the door open, and I was genuinely confused. This caused the final breakdown of the marriage as she now had proof that her intuition of his cheating was correct. When she confronted him, he left the house with his things, and we found out that he had taken all of the money out of the bank account, leaving us with nothing.

Around this time I remember my mother put my brother and me in the car and said we were going to the lawyer's office. She had a pile of papers that she was fumbling with in her hands. I know now that it was to sign divorce papers. She wasn't crying, but there was an energy of desperation that I could not escape. I remember my brother and me remaining very silent. It was the same energy of us having to leave under the cover of night, running from my belligerent father many times before. I was 8 years old and all I knew was that the lawyer's office smelled like old leather, and nobody seemed happy. In the waiting room, she opened her purse and showed us a handful of leaves from a plant around our neighborhood that she had always told us to stay away from because it was poisonous. She turned to us and said, "I plan on eating these in there; tell your father that he pushed me to this point." We looked around, unsure how to respond as she entered a room and closed the door behind her.

Shortly thereafter, the door opened, and she walked out. A sense of relief enveloped us, but I also remember feeling extremely stressed and sad. Through this and other moments like it I learned by example that having a toxic life and making dramatic expressions was normal. I now believe some of her actions piqued my interest in the idea of suicide. This was the first time I recall thinking: "Oh, I can check myself out of here. That doesn't sound too bad. Eat something and fall asleep and take the pain away?" Again, the young mind skips over all the other horrid details. But still, it cemented the thought that I could choose an escape hatch when life became too hard. I filed this thought inside my mind in a folder titled, "Open any time life gets too hard."

Pretty quickly, both of my parents were in other relationships. My mother never physically abused me. Her form of abuse was being distant while she focused on her various forms of numbing. I longed for hair brushing, back rubs, storytelling, hugs, and positive reinforcement. She was energetically comatose, and it felt like she wasn't present even if she physically was. My father was incredibly self-centered as well, and taking care of his children was not a primary concern unless it somehow helped him. He had been married six times already, with at least four other children he'd left behind before they turned 2 years old. I was living with my mother and brother, and my mother had custody of us, and my father was to pay child support. He devised a plan to get out of paying by seeking full custody of me. He met a sweet woman with her own two daughters and got remarried, and they all wanted me to be a part of their family. My mother was enjoying her new life and was rarely around anyway, and my father told me that he wanted me with his new family and that he had quit drinking. I was nearly 9 years old and believed I was finally getting what I wanted. I agreed to move in with him based on this new fantasy family, and my father got custody of me for the next four years.

Within weeks, he was back to drinking, and my stepmother fled with her daughters after a violent night. I remember the look of shock and sorrow on her face when she realized what he turned into. They tried to take me too, but he stripped me away from their arms and said, "Not her; she is mine." I never heard from them again.

My father realized that the storyline of being a single dad to a cute little girl could land a lot of women who wanted to mother us. I became female bait. He would often leave me home alone for long periods, sometimes with strangers who barely knew me. Other times, I would sit in the back of a bar all night until he was ready to leave. I still can't smell Shirley Temples without getting sick. He even taught me how to drive to avoid getting more DUIs. It was a time where they still let you drive home or sleep it off in jail if you were caught driving intoxicated. I was a very good driver, and having this responsibility made me feel like I was contributing somehow. All of this helped me hone my self-preservation skills. I became a mood-changing chameleon so I could adjust to any situation. I would wonder, "Can I make them laugh? Shall I sing, dance, clean something, or even run away for a while?" My father would make me bartend for him and his friends. He drank a Cuba Libre with rum, coke, and a slice of lime. It sounded way fancier than it is.

Miraculously, I had the wherewithal to continue to take myself to school; it was my only refuge, and I cherished learning, even though the chaos at home made it hard for me to concentrate and focus. I saw school as my path out of that life, but I always felt like an outsider who was a step behind. I remember thinking that so much of this world was beautiful—all the skies, the trees, the rivers, but it was a mistake that I was here. I often thought about ending my life, but the fear and anguish over it made me cry. I thought of never seeing my mother again and how she'd feel when she learned about my death. My empathy for her would often stop my ideation because, even as a child, I knew I didn't want to do that to her. Even though she was not the attentive and affectionate mother I craved, I loved her. Gratefully, my love for my mother helped keep me here. Somehow, I knew she had already been through too much; you could see it in her eyes, and my heart ached at the sight of it.

I had a dog that I loved, Satchmo. He was a black-haired poodle-schnauzer mix and came into the world around the same time I did. I always thought of him as an angel sent to protect me. Sadly, I was unable to protect my treasured pet. One day, my father stabbed Satchmo with a broom under the couch repeatedly because he went to the bathroom on the carpet after being left inside all day. I did everything I could to stop my dad, but Satchmo was never the same after that. This was the origin of my anger toward those who hurt animals, and a zealous nature ignited in me at 12 years old. It is interesting that it was easier for me to feel a sense of protection and compassion toward Satchmo than to give myself the same.

The last day I lived with my father, I was swimming at a friend's house. Another friend called me while I was there and warned, "Your dad is going door-to-door looking for you, and he looks pissed, don't go home." He was on a rampage—supposedly because he thought I stole a considerable amount of marijuana. He didn't know that I stayed far away from pot as it reminded me of him.

Instead of going home, I walked around town as long as possible. Once I was too tired to keep going, I snuck back into the house to sleep. I hid in the corner of my waterbed where the plastic and wood separated and put the covers over me to camouflage myself. He must have realized I was there and woke me up and dragged me out of bed by my hair. I got free momentarily; he had a bad case of gout which slowed him down. I ran to the phone and called my mother, begging her to get me, something I had not done before. She lived about forty-five minutes away.

I was in a fetal position in a corner of the house while my dad repeatedly kicked me. I saw a shadow through a doorway as I slipped in and out of consciousness. I don't know how, but my mom got me out, and I left there for good without my dear Satchmo. My mom tried to get Satchmo for me, but my dad would not release him. I heard he left him strapped to the back of a U-Haul truck and another dog attacked him, and he died.

I didn't see or speak to my father again until I was eighteen. I had moved to Los Angeles where he was also living at the time, and he sent me $250 and told me to buy myself a puppy. Maybe this was his way of making an apology? In 2008, I called to tell him I was getting married. He answered, "Well, have a nice life." My heart sank again; that was the last time I spoke to him.

I learned there had been only one person at his funeral. I did not bask in this information. A few years ago, I drove to the Naval Cemetery in Riverside, California. I lay down on his patch of grass with a handwritten note, a picture of our family, and flowers. I told him about my life, marriages, happy and sad times, and how proud he would be of me. I felt a light of love all around me. I don't know if it was coming from me or him, but something powerful had shifted for both of our souls. This helped to release the traumatic triggers. Now and then, I get a sense of him being grateful that I have set him free in my heart. A big part of my healing has been understanding the circumstances when I was younger and giving myself plenty of room to explore the depths of how this contributed to my suicidal thoughts.

My Brother Johnny, Taken Too Soon

My brother was not my father's biological child (which I didn't learn until I was much older), so he lived with my mother. When my mother rescued me from my father, I went back to live with her for a few years until I turned fourteen. I was under the same roof as my brother again, but he was a wild teenager, and I rarely saw him. He was five years older than me, practically a grown-up in the seventies, where kids were allowed to roam parentless for days. They used to have television commercials that came on at 10:00 pm that said, "Do you know where your children are?" Parents had to be reminded they had kids. It was a different time.

I loved being with Johnny, but this did not last long because a few years later, he moved to Southern California for truck-driving school. Shortly after arriving in California, Johnny was involved in a motorcycle accident that left him with a traumatic brain injury, causing permanent damage. To this day, it was the only time I've seen my mother cry. When we got to the hospital in California, we found the priest reading him his rites. I remember that just after he'd come out of his coma, he looked at us, grabbed his feeding tube, and started pulling it out, saying, "I want to die. Why didn't I die? I can't do this. Please kill me." I ran over and tried to stop him, screaming for the nurse, who had to sedate him and tie his arms to his sides. He knew the road to recovery would be hard, and he did not want to go through it.

He spent an entire year in that hospital. After he left, friends visited at first, but eventually they moved on with their busy lives and stopped coming around. Johnny said, "I see the world living and growing around me, but I'm not a part of it." He felt he had no future left, a familiar feeling among those who are suicidal. I wanted to help him, but he became resentful of me, a seemingly young, healthy girl filled with friends and adventure. Johnny drank himself to death at the age of twenty-nine in his own painfully slow, suicidal act. A few nights before his passing, he asked me, "Is there any way that I might live?" I answered, "Well, you would need to stop drinking." He said, "That's okay . . . never mind. Can you play 'Free Bird' at the funeral for me?"

A Lotus Flower Blooms Above the Mud

I was in a fight for my life, and I had to find my unique path to healing. Even though my story's specific content will differ from yours,

I tell it in the hope that it resonates with you so you can find your healing path and know that I deeply understand.

When I felt I had healed my suicidal ideation, I was impassioned to share what I learned in order to help others. Once Dr. Amelia Kelley and the Swedenborg Foundation joined me on this journey, I got to work, filled with anticipation. However, my theories would be put to the ultimate test while I was writing this book: the same day I signed the publishing deal, my mother had her first serious medical incident—a heart attack. I had just moved to Montana from California with my fiancé of three years. I had to leave immediately. Once in California again, I realized how out of place I felt in Montana. It didn't feel like home.

My fiancé had recently started acting strangely, convincing me to purchase large-ticket items and put them in his name. When I returned to Montana a week later, most of my belongings had been wiped out, and all my photo albums and framed family pictures had been destroyed.

A note on the counter said he had met a girl and was now with her. He would not pay for the lease or expenses, or return the items I had purchased. I had to get a lawyer and we reached a settlement that was skewed in my ex-fiancé's favor. However, I wanted to leave this isolated, snow-covered place and return to my mother, and to everything and everyone I loved.

Fortunately, a friend offered me a space in Topanga Canyon, California, while I looked for something permanent. As I sat in this small trailer alone with my two dogs, at the age of fifty-three, reeling from betrayal, every part of my life felt chaotic and hanging by a thread—except this book and the drive to get it into the hands of each person who needed it. I had to push through the mud like a lotus flower, and continue to bloom. There was one massive difference this time: *I did not or could not hold a single or lasting suicidal thought*. It was as if a switch flipped that could never be turned on again. I had this deep feeling: "That is not you anymore."

I now know that it needed to happen this way. Before putting this book into the world, I needed to be confident that even in the midst of personal challenges and turmoil, I had eradicated suicidal ideation from my being. To ace this final test, which is what life is to me (a series of lessons where the answers are not revealed quickly), I had to do the work, dig in, apply the tools, practice, study, and most important, have faith. I was actively using this book as I wrote it. That is, in part, what makes it unique.

You can achieve this as well. By working intensely with the intelligence of your being and committing yourself to dutifully accept this journey and the opportunity to heal, you can get to the other side of pain and find joy again. I know how this rugged road can feel. As you heal, you will find hidden treasures within yourself that you didn't know existed. But this is only possible if you are still here. ♡

FINDING PURPOSE

In the 1946 book *Man's Search for Meaning*,[5] psychologist and Holocaust survivor Viktor Frankl explored how, despite life's worst circumstances, having a sense of purpose or meaning can liberate us from emotional pain and various forms of suffering—suicidal ideation included. For some, meaning can come in the form of the work you do; for others, it is found within relationships. For Gina, her desire to help those suffering from suicidal ideation is part of what has given her own life meaning and joy. Work is a common conduit for meaning; however, it is not the only nor the most powerful one.

Another way to create purpose and meaning is through learning, which happens anytime we try to find ways to overcome the challenges of being human. Choosing to pick up this book and apply what is taught within it is a decision to find purpose amidst the pain that suicidality creates.

As you continue to read about Gina's survival and rebirth, you will also be given the opportunity to learn research-supported tools and

5. Viktor E Frankl, *Man's Search for Meaning* (1959. Reprint, Boston: Beacon Press, 2006).

healing practices to address passive suicidality (daydreaming, thinking, or wishing for your death without a specific plan in place) and active suicidality (thinking of specific ways to end one's own life and a reduced fear of death) that helped her find joy and peace. ♡

Building Support and Purpose Exercise

Commitment can serve as one of the most important protective factors when considering suicidal thoughts. Relationships, a job, a goal of some kind, our own faith, or a beloved pet can all remind us of a purpose outside of ourselves, quieting the hum of suicidality. I often ask my clients experiencing suicidal thoughts to commit to meeting me at their next session. We will set life work to do between sessions as an anchor to something beyond their suicidality. Take a moment here to consider any protective factors or life work you have and list them below (note that if any of this brings up intense feelings, you are empowered to skip this altogether).

Relationships (i.e., children, spouse, parents, chosen family):

_____

_____

_____

Pets or animals you are responsible for:

_____

_____

_____

Goals you are working toward (or want to):

_____

_____

_____

Volunteer or charity ideas that fill your heart:

_____

_____

_____

Cultural or spiritual beliefs about suicide:

_____

_____

_____

Identifying who you feel comfortable speaking to can be challenging at times, especially if you haven't experienced support in these ways. The following questions are designed to help you work through this process.

Who is someone who has helped me (even in a small way) move in a positive direction, and what did they do?

_____

_____

_____

If, at any point while reading this book, my ideation increases or the desire to commit suicide becomes unbearable, I will commit to calling my support people above, or I can contact the following agency or mental health professionals:

_____

_____

_____

Some people find a therapist to be integral in healing from suicidal ideation. When therapy serves as a place to receive support and validation, rather than solely as a place to fix problems, it has true value in managing suicidal thoughts. Finding the right therapist, or alternative healer, is a very individualized experience, and you deserve to be specific about what you want and need.

Search for a therapist at psychologytoday.com or betterhelp.com.

MAKING SELF-LOVE PART OF YOUR COMMITMENT

> Love is our very life, and the quality of our love determines the quality of our life. —Emanuel Swedenborg, Secrets of Heaven 3539:4

I lived too much in my mind, and not in my heart. If anyone else had lived in my mind during the times when I was suicidal, they, too, would have been suicidal. Nobody could sustain that level of self-hatred and negative abuse and feel as if they were thriving. I struggled to understand why my internal monologue consistently communicated cruel things. I had to rewrite my program. I committed to talking to myself in kinder ways in that very moment. If a negative thought pattern came up, I imagined a STOP sign in my head, literally stopping the words. When I removed the self-shame spirals, it created room for good things to come in. Soon, the loving thoughts pushed out the bad ones. Eventually, with practice, I gained control of how I spoke to myself and how I let others speak to me. It was a 360-degree turnaround.

Now that I am on the other side, I can see that version of myself in those moments of total despair with compassion. I imagine crawling into the room, gently cradling my former self in my arms and wiping my own tears and whispering beautiful messages of hope and love until that version of me feels better. It's helped me to remove the painful energy around those times so I can reframe them as a time of healing. I can look back at those moments with love and understanding instead of shame.

I had to learn how to mother myself not just by getting my needs met but also by learning how to love everything about me while being able to recognize the things I wanted to adjust. Finding ways to practice self-love is one of the most critical commitments on this healing journey. Even picking up this book is an act of self-love. This practice is not easy, but I am here to tell you that I understand. It's worth a valiant effort for yourself. Practice self-love repeatedly and it will become your superpower.

If you find yourself engaging in negative self-talk while reading this book, pay attention to what triggers you. The goal is to remain at least neutral, curious, and open. Tread carefully to avoid the mental quicksand. Although circumstances may shatter you for a moment, and you will inevitably feel deep grief as that is part of being human, you can evolve into a stronger person for the experience. If you love and mother yourself through it, these moments can become a source of strength.

My Daily Process

An ex-boyfriend used to ask me, "Are there evil squirrels juggling knives in your head?" It would make me laugh, but it gives a visual of how our busy minds can work. As soon as I wake up, I have a choice whether to let my thoughts dictate my day or whether to engage in the healing and grounding work I have called "my process." To support your healing journey, I want to share mine with you, perhaps to elicit ideas or to help you recognize some of the positive techniques you are already personally using.

Morning Practice

- First, hug yourself and others around you if that is your situation. Stretch your arms and legs out and look at your hands and feet (if you can), and notice that they are alive. Imagine what they might do or create on this day ahead of you. Look around the room and notice your space and any other living beings and offer them energetic love, including your partner, children, family members, animals, and even your living plants. Say with deep conviction and power, "Hello,

I love you." The word "Hello" actually holds great power in its spiritual intention. We will address this in later meditations.

- Play meditation music on low so it's not overpowering but lays a calming vibration throughout your space.

- Invite the phrase (either out loud or internally): "I am so grateful and excited that I get to . . ." and list the people, projects, and things you will be interacting with that day. This puts a vibration of high energy around the entire day and for all those you mention.

Midday Practice

- When you experience tension, anxiety, or fear, remind yourself that you have everything you need to remain centered in your own energy. Invite the phrase (either out loud or internally): "I am anxious about this _____ _____, but I have all the tools to succeed. No matter what happens, it will be a valuable experience in my life." Even if doubt arises, you can speak these words to increase a positive vibration.

Evening Practice

- Take three deep breaths in and out; then, reflect on what happened that day and either speak, imagine, or journal about these events. Checking in with yourself increases self-awareness and enhances the ability to pay attention to lessons provided throughout your day. Honor yourself for being present and trying to move through your life. Finding things that work for you as an individual to close out the day is important. You might want to do a crossword, read, or take a short walk. Whatever it is, try to find at least one habitual thing you like to do. The schedule helps to ground us especially when we are in moments of depression or other negative states.

Energetic Movement

We as human bodies are constantly in motion. Even in death, if you look at our cells under a microscope, there is still movement. This can be felt as well in the body in times of stress and even in times of joy. For example, I have a ball of energy in my back that vibrates subtly when I am doing healthy or positive things for myself; over time, it has gotten stronger and stronger. Now, it is constantly communicating with me. I'll be interviewing someone for my podcast, and if we are talking about a very important subject, I can feel the ball in my back start to move. It is as if it is telling me that this subject and person are of high vibration, that this is good energy, and that I should continue to work with this person. It also tells me if I need to create distance if it goes dormant around someone—I realize then I shouldn't pursue a relationship or project with that person or company. This ball of energy was dormant until about four years ago when I reached in my healing journey **Phase 5: Confidence,** which we will discuss in Part 2. Before this level of healing, I was so heavy in my energy with the thoughts of leaving this Earth that I was not able to feel deeply.

You too have the ability to feel this energy in your body. To put it into practice: Close your eyes and sit or lie down. Feel your breath coming from your diaphragm, moving it up through your lungs as they expand and out of your nose and mouth. Can you feel any subtle phenomena around this? Is the air cold or warm? Do you feel sensations anywhere in the body? Go to those places, and when you breathe in and out, imagine the air going right to that spot, filling it with energy and a beautiful light filled with any color you want. If you struggle to connect with this feeling, you may want to consider what you are putting into your body. Your ecosystem may be trying to tell you something. Perhaps you had too much coffee or sugar? If you are still struggling to connect energetically, you might consider if you are moving enough throughout the day. While everyone has different capabilities, any movement is a great way to push through stuck energy. Whether your movements are subtle or more intense, think about your feelings as you move. Can you feel your blood pumping through your heart? Your limbs? Connect with your body in gratitude as you move, whichever way you choose and are capable of. I ask my students, "How often have you met a depressed surfer?"

It's rare because they move, feel, and connect to nature, and the muck falls off! Whether speaking kindly to yourself throughout the day, journaling, or feeling your shifting energy, the most important thing is to remain holistically connected to your true self and the ability to feel the warmth and energetic shift of self-love.

Earlier in my story, I explained that I used to act like a chameleon to change my personality so I could meet others where they were. I did this to fit in and not be rejected or abandoned. I do not do this anymore. I am myself constantly, and if it's not a fit for another person, then I move on. I don't take it personally anymore. I love myself. I feel it, and I believe it. Later in this book, Dr. Kelley will share the entire framework for learning about the Self (with a capital S) and the various parts that make up your entire internal system as described by the Internal Family Systems approach. She will guide you in recognizing them, learning from them, and working with them when healing from suicidal ideation. For now, we want to share an exercise to tune into the love that is available as a resource within your own spirit. This resource might not always feel available, so the following exercise can help to bring awareness to its presence and help identify what is blocking the way to our perception of it. ♋

Self-Love Measurement Exercise

- Imagine a gauge in front of you. It can look like a speedometer ranging from 0 to 100.

- With your eyes closed, and focusing on the image of the gauge, ask yourself: "How much self-love do I have presently for myself?"

- The first number that comes to mind is the right one because that is your intuitive self communicating. There is no need to judge or criticize the number; it is simply a way for you to connect with your authentic self.

- Write this number in a journal or here: _____.

- As you work through this book and fight for yourself in a positive way, your self-love number will likely increase. Awareness is helpful when making change so it can help to re-rate your self-love each time you sit down to read and record your progress.

THE POWER OF MEDITATION

Meditation is one of the most accessible and cost-effective, yet under-utilized ways to overcome suicidal thoughts. In a study conducted on college students (who are a high-risk group, with suicide being the fourth-leading cause of death for individuals aged fifteen to twenty-nine years)[6] who were experiencing high suicidal ideation, the use of Brief Mindfulness Meditation was examined as a coping mechanism. The study found that after one month of practice, not only did the participants' ideation drop significantly, but their sleep also improved, and saliva swabs showed reduced levels of the stress hormone cortisol.

To ensure that the experience of meditation is positive for those suffering from suicidal ideation, it is important to recognize that certain forms of meditation can heighten despair. For example, Vipassana, or insight meditation, is intended as an inward journey of acknowledging any negative feelings, pain, or blockages to achieve healing and empowerment. While this form of meditation is powerful and has beneficial purposes, it is not well suited to counter suicidal thoughts, depression, or anguish until you've built up a strong anchor of love within yourself. That is why in this book we are focusing on what in our experience are the most beneficial forms of meditation for combatting suicidality. This includes calming, grounding, guided, and relaxation meditations.

Finding a teacher to support your journey with meditation can also help ensure that your meditation practice promotes healing and safety. You may choose to find a group or teacher in your community.

6. World Health Organization, "Suicide Prevention," https://www.who.int/health-topics/suicide.

> *Our mind, meaning our volition and discernment, is our spirit, and the spirit is a person. Our spirit has a pulse and breathing just as the body does. The pulse and breathing of the spirit within us flows into the pulse and breathing of our body and causes them.*
> —*Emanuel Swedenborg,* Divine Love and Wisdom *390*

How to Put It into Practice

Many clients I work with struggle with the idea of "thinking of nothing" and fear that they will "fail" at meditating. I would like to reassure you that meditation is not a "one-size-fits-all" practice, and there are many ways to adjust the experience to fit your needs. In this first chapter, we are exploring what it means to love yourself enough to stay alive by using meditation focused on self-love and confidence.

Meditation is a powerful way to ease negative self-talk and suffering. A study conducted on survivors of trauma with post-traumatic stress disorder (PTSD) found that three weeks of mindfulness-based stress reduction not only reduced negative symptom presentation, but it also significantly increased perceived self-worth.[7] The practice also led to a marked increase in cortical matter (thickness in the outer layer of the brain) in the prefrontal cortex where decision making, executive functioning (the ability to accomplish tasks effectively even under pressure), and emotion regulation are centered.[8]

Some of the more difficult moments of suicidal thinking or planning are done in the depths of pain, suffering, and despair. But if your brain were trained to handle these emotions more effectively, you could employ coping skills more often. Ironically, the worse we feel, the less we tend to use coping skills—even though this is when we truly need them.

---

7. Jenna E. Boyd, Ruth A. Lanius, and Margaret C. McKinnon, "Mindfulness-based Treatments for Posttraumatic Stress Disorder: A Review of the Treatment Literature and Neurobiological Evidence," Journal of Psychiatry and Neuroscience 43, no. 1 (2018): 7–25.
8. Sara W. Lazar et al. "Meditation Experience Is Associated with Increased Cortical Thickness," *Neuroreport* 16, no. 17 (2005): 1893–1897, accessed September 1, 2023, https://.ncbi.nlm.nih.gov/pmc/articles/PMC1361002/.

When using the various meditation practices offered in the book, it can help to approach your practice with compassion and to consider the following:

- Be gentle with yourself when your mind wanders. It's less about trying to stop thoughts from happening than it is to shift your relationship toward them.

- Find a comfortable but well-supported position. This may mean lying down, sitting in a chair with your feet firmly planted on the floor, or sitting cross-legged on a supportive cushion.

- Moving is okay, but the more you can settle in and calm your mind, the less likely you will feel the need to move or fidget.

- You can practice in silence, or you can choose to ground yourself in the present with ambient meditation-style music.

- Your breath is a fantastic anchor. Some tools include counting your breaths, saying "in" and "out" as you breathe, or imagining your breath descending and ascending like an elevator.

- When you have thoughts or your mind wanders, just witness them and allow them to float by.

- If closing your eyes is triggering, you can find a Drishti gaze (point of focus) in front of you.

- Finally, know that each "sit" differs, and no two are alike. ♡

Courageous Heart Opening/Centering Meditation

(2–5 minutes)

You can do this meditation in a quiet place for deeper reflection, or if you are in a state where you need assistance and cannot be alone, you can do it with a trusted person. This meditation can also be used as a grounding method if you are triggered or emotionally dysregulated.

It can be done in silence or with the presence of calming music, tones, or nature sounds.

- Sit, stand, or lie down, based on your current needs and comfort.

- Become aware of your breath. Deepen it and notice it coming in and going out.

- Close your eyes if you are in a place where you can (though it is not necessary).

- Now, take one hand and place it over your heart. Take the other hand and place it right above your belly button onto what is called the solar plexus.

- As you inhale, imagine breathing in fresh, new, life-giving oxygen.

- As you exhale, imagine breathing out any feelings that you would like to release.

- Visualize your breath entering the front of the heart and exiting from the back of the heart.

- Imagine someone or something that brings you joy.

- Next, conjure feelings of self-love and appreciation by imagining a bright color (such as green, blue, pink, yellow, orange, or gold) shining all around you.

- Say "hello" and your name out loud if you can. Repeat this at least three times.

- Sense now that your hands and arms are holding you with deep love and fondness.

- When you feel calm, or are ready to end your practice, notice the sensations of the room around you and gently open your eyes.

- If you like, end by turning the corners of your mouth upward and thank yourself for the time in meditation.

- If you feel compelled to journal any thoughts, visions, or emotions, you can do so below.

Notes on your experience trying the meditation:

_____

_____

_____

 GOING FORWARD WITH CARE & COMMITMENT
This first chapter was meant as a root system by which to grow throughout this book. We explored why talking about suicidality openly and honestly is the foundation to healing because we cannot overcome what we do not know. We also discussed why finding purpose and self-love is crucial when overcoming suicidal ideation. Learning how to practice self-love using meditation and mindfulness are just some of the methods you will learn, and with each new chapter, the skills presented will enhance your ability to heal and grow.

As Gina unfolds her personal experience, you will be given opportunities to reflect more on your own story. We encourage you to always put self-care at the forefront. One way to prioritize self-care is to take your time while reading this book. If feelings of resistance, insecurity, or overwhelm occur while reading the material, know this is normal. Embracing the potential of an unknown opportunity can be scary but also positive and powerful. When we are at the brink of change, our body and mind may feel alarmed, so we would like to encourage you to try something. If you feel that flush of fear when letting go of old thoughts or coping patterns, know that your body is simply signaling that something important is happening. Recognize this with curiosity and, if possible, acceptance.

Chapter 2: The Impact

If we believed that—as is truly the case—everything good and true comes from the Lord and everything evil and false comes from hell, then we would not claim the goodness as our own and make it self-serving or claim the evil as our own and make ourselves guilty of it. —Emanuel Swedenborg, Divine Providence 320

 OVERCOMING SUICIDAL IDEATION includes understanding and recognizing some of the greatest risk factors. At the top of this list is the presence of PTSD and its co-occurring disorders (depression and anxiety), as well as substance abuse, chronic health issues and medical illness, and poverty. In this chapter, we will explore some of these risk factors, how they presented for Gina, and how these issues may have manifested in your own life.

As you read this chapter, it is important to understand that the experience of these risk factors and their presence in an individual's life develop on account of our burdened cultures and not as a personal failing on the part of the person suffering.

MYTHS

Though suicide is not always predictable, it can be preventable. An important component to prevention is dispelling unhelpful beliefs and myths that impact our attitudes toward suicide—doing so helps eliminate barriers that prevent those suffering from asking for help, as well as educating and empowering those who can offer support to them.

Common Myths Around Suicide

The following illustrates some of the most harmful myths about suicide. These myths, which have grown to become taboo topics, prevent accurate and helpful dialogue from occurring that would bring about real and lasting change for those who struggle with suicidal thoughts or persons healing from suicide loss. We encourage you to read through them and contemplate whether the important people in your life have said or thought some of these things. It may also be helpful to ask yourself how you feel about each statement. After reflecting, take a moment to journal your responses. Normalizing these hard conversations and debunking these societal myths can make it more likely someone will approach survivors or those who have mentioned previous ideation of suicide by listening, asking questions, and providing empathy and support.

Myth: Suicide can't be prevented.
Fact: According to the Centers for Disease Control, suicide is preventable (yet unpredictable at times) and requires strategies at all levels of society.[9] Everyone can help prevent suicide by learning the warning signs. It is a product of genetics, mental health issues, and environmental risk factors. Interventions that treat psychiatric and substance use illnesses could save lives.

---

9. "Prevention Strategies: A Comprehensive Public Health Approach to Suicide Prevention Can Decrease Risk," The Centers for Disease Control, accessed April 9, 2024, https://.cdc.gov/suicide/prevention/index.html.

Myth: People who take their own lives are selfish, cowardly, or weak.
Fact: Though it can be difficult to understand, people who die by suicide would prefer another choice, and it is not intended to harm any other person. Often, people who die of suicide experience significant emotional pain and find it difficult to consider different views or see a way out of their situation.

Myth: Talking about suicide increases the chance a person will act on it.
Fact: Research shows[10] that talking openly about suicide, in a safe and supportive manner, makes it less likely to occur and more likely someone will seek treatment and potentially find alternative options for coping with pain and trauma.

Myth: People who talk about suicide are just attention seekers.
Fact: Those who are willing to talk about suicide are actually quite brave, and their efforts to seek support and help should be honored.

Myth: Teenagers and college students are the most at risk for suicide.
Fact: According to the Mayo Clinic,[11] the suicide rate for this age group is below the national average, and suicide risk increases with age. The age group with the highest suicide rate in the U.S. is men and women between 45 and 64. Though particular groups may be at higher risk, suicide is a problem among all ages and groups.

Myth: Suicide occurs without warning.
Fact: Almost all suicide is preceded by warning signs, and it is important to understand what these signs are and educate others about

10. Substance Abuse and Mental Health Services Administration (SAMHSA), *Treatment for Suicidal Ideation, Self-harm, and Suicide Attempts Among Youth*, SAMHSA Publication No. PEP20-06-01-002, Rockville, MD: National Mental Health and Substance Use Policy Laboratory, Substance Abuse and Mental Health Services Administration, 2020.
11. Pravesh Sharma, "8 Common Myths About Suicide," *Mayo Clinic Health System*, December 20, 2021, https://.mayoclinichealthsystem.org/hometown-health/speaking-of-health/8-common-myths-about-suicide.

them. To learn more about potential signs, reference the **5 Phases of Suicidal Ideation** in Chapter 3.

Myth: Alternative therapies, talk therapy, and medications don't work.
Fact: These treatments do work, and research shows[12] that a number of suicides occur when someone is without these supports. Different treatments work for everyone, so finding what feels like the best fit is most helpful.

Myth: Ideation is shameful.
Fact: It is not abnormal to experience suicidal thoughts. As death will occur for all of us, it is common to imagine or contemplate one's own death. Whether it escalates to intent and planning is related to trauma, mental health, and a host of complex factors, none of which warrant shame.

Myth: Someone who is going through or has experienced a suicidal crisis cannot help others.
Fact: Some of the most profound healers are wounded and have been able to integrate their past experiences of trauma to help and empower others. The important factor is to make sure you are well-supported in your healing journey and have spent time processing certain issues prior to helping others.

The Relationship Between Self-Injury and Suicide

A common misunderstanding about self-injury—such as cutting, burning, scratching, or hitting oneself—is that it is always a warning sign of suicidal behaviors. The confusion makes sense since the two can look very similar. Understanding how they differ and how they are related is an important part of suicide prevention.

12. Evan M. Kleiman and Richard T. Liu, "Social Support as a Protective Factor in Suicide: Findings from Two Nationally Representative Samples," *Journal of Affective Disorders* 150, no. 2 (2013): 540–545, accessed August 22, 2023, https://doi.org/10.1016%2Fj.jad.2013.01.033.

Differences

There are several differences between self-injury and suicide. One of the more important differences is the intent. With self-injury, the purpose is to feel better, whereas with suicide, the purpose is to end a feeling, or a life, altogether. The ways each of these acts are carried out differ greatly as well. Methods used in self-injury typically damage the surface of the body and are not intended to create long-term damage. Suicide-related behaviors tend to be much more lethal and more often focus on permanently damaging the internal body that sustains life.

While psychological pain is significant in both instances, the level of distress that occurs during self-injury is markedly less than when someone is considering suicide. If anything, some use self-injury to avoid attempting suicide, at times as a risky coping mechanism. This can be confusing for people who want to support the person who is hurting themselves, and knowing when to be concerned is often a question.

Someone who has been self-harming can usually identify a variety of feelings and cognitive structures about their actions. The person may even be able to describe what they are doing and why. With someone who is actively suicidal, there will be a presence of cognitive constriction, otherwise known as black-or-white thinking, where everything is either good or bad. This way of thinking is a barrier to finding effective ways to heal and is commonly connected to major depressive disorder, which increases the risk of suicide.

According to Janis Whitlock and Elizabeth Lloyd-Richardson, authors of *Healing Self-Injury: A Compassionate Guide for Parents and Other Loved Ones*,[13] other factors that can place someone at greater risk of moving from self-injury to suicide include:

- Greater family conflict and poor relationship with parents

- More than twenty lifetime non-suicidal, self-injury incidents

13. Janis Whitlock and Elizabeth Lloyd-Richardson, *Healing Self-injury: A Compassionate Guide for Parents and Other Loved Ones* (Oxford University Press, 2019).

- Psychological distress within the past thirty days
- A history of emotional or sexual trauma
- Greater feelings of hopelessness
- Self-hatred
- Wanting to feel something
- High impulsivity and engagement in risky behaviors
- Substance use
- A diagnosis of major depressive disorder or PTSD

What is important to understand is that when someone is suffering, the more connected they feel with their support system, the less likely self-injury behaviors will escalate to suicidal intent and action. If you believe you are struggling with self-injury, we encourage you to reach out to a medical or mental health professional or perhaps speak to one of the support people in your safety plan. Trying to lean into some of the coping skills provided throughout this book, while using the urge wave to let the desire to self-harm pass, is another powerful way to heal and remain safe while doing so. If you want to learn this now, please go to page 137.

RISK FACTORS

While every person's experience is unique, there are certain universal experiences that can increase the risk of suicidal thoughts for most people. Understanding what these common experiences are and how they can increase the risk of suicidality is useful knowledge for addressing these issues if they arise. Understanding risks around suicide can also validate your experience, knowing that others may encounter difficulties when facing the same challenges.

Trauma

According to the National Council for Mental Wellbeing,[14] 70 percent of adults in the U.S. will experience some type of traumatic experience in the course of their lives. That comes to 223.4 million people as of 2023. Trauma can take many appearances. The following are some terms to help simplify the matter and help you recognize your own past traumatic experiences.

> **Acute (Single-Incident) Trauma:** includes physical or sexual assault and abuse, motor accidents, combat and war, endangerment of first responders and law enforcement, death of a loved one, natural disasters (floods, earthquakes, and fires), and being diagnosed with a life-threatening condition.

> **Complex (Chronic) Trauma:** involves multiple events with interpersonal threats that often occur over a period of time (commonly in childhood or within close intimate relationships). Such events may include abuse, neglect, interpersonal violence, community violence, racism, discrimination, and the ongoing effects of war.

Another common way to describe trauma is with the terms "Little t" versus "Big T" trauma. The term "little" seems to imply it has less impact or potential for harm. This simply is not true. The main difference between the two is that Big T trauma includes either witnessing the endangerment of others (such as being present at a shooting even if you are not personally targeted) as well as personally experiencing such events (either through assault or abuse or as a result of natural disasters). Let's explore these two variations a bit further.

Little t trauma typically does not involve violence or disaster but does create significant distress. It is a disruption to life and can compound in its effect over time. Little t trauma can come in the form of positive or harmful stressors. Examples of harmful forms of Little t

---

14. *How Common is Trauma*, The National Council for Mental Wellbeing, accessed April 9, 2024, https://.thenationalcouncil.org/wp-content/uploads/2022/08/Trauma-infographic.pdf.

trauma include a breakup, the death of a pet, moving, losing a job, getting bullied, or being rejected by a friend group.

Examples of subjectively positive Little t trauma that can cause traumatic disruption to one's life include the stress around starting a new job, moving to a new town, or even becoming a parent. For this reason, it is helpful to be specific when exploring this form of trauma. Understanding the impact of trauma in its many forms is completely relative to the person's past and present life experiences.

As was explored briefly in the section on complex trauma, someone's life may not be in danger when they are being emotionally neglected. For this reason, one could argue that *stonewalling* (a form of silent treatment in which someone refuses to communicate with another person and withdraws to create distance, causing frustration and loneliness for the person being targeted)[15] is in fact a form of Little t trauma. What this means is that all forms of trauma should be taken seriously as there is no measure of "how much trauma" should or can cause suicidal ideation as well as other mental health issues.

Big T trauma refers to instances where your life or that of a loved one may be endangered, such as by sexual or physical assault, combat, serious injuries with long-term impact, and near-death experiences.

Experiencing trauma does not determine whether someone develops PTSD; rather, it is determined by how one copes and reacts after the event has occurred. Certain factors make it more likely for someone to develop PTSD. One example is whether the person is able to mobilize and get themselves out of danger, thus completing the trauma cycle, leading to a potential feeling of self-agency. Resilience (the ability to withstand and recover from adversity) also plays a role in whether someone develops PTSD and whether they are more likely to attempt suicide, as 27 percent of people with PTSD make at least one attempt.[16]

15. "The Four Horsemen: Stonewalling," The Gottman Institute, accessed March 30, 2024, https://www.gottman.com/blog/the-four-horsemen-stonewalling/.
16. "The Link Between PTSD and Suicide," Psych Central, accessed April 9, 2024, https://psychcentral.com/ptsd/ptsd-suicide.

While the nature of trauma varies greatly, when PTSD does develop (outside the first 30 days after a trauma event), the following symptoms are most common:

Re-experiencing	◊ Flashbacks ◊ Bad dreams ◊ Frightening thoughts
Avoidance	◊ Staying away from places, events, or objects that are reminders of the experience ◊ Avoiding thoughts or feelings related to the traumatic event
Arousal and reactivity	◊ Being easily startled ◊ Feeling tense or "on edge" ◊ Having difficulty sleeping and/or having angry outbursts
Cognition and mood	◊ Trouble remembering key features of the traumatic event ◊ Negative thoughts about oneself or the world ◊ Distorted feelings like guilt or blame ◊ Loss of interest in enjoyable activities

While trauma is universal, research has found that those with complex or Big T trauma are at greater risk of struggling with suicidal ideation. This is because these forms of trauma disrupt our sense of safety with others and the world around us. Considering that healthy relationships are a major component to resilience, and resilience reduces suicidal ideation, this explains part of why trauma increases the prevalence of suicidality.

The hopeful news is that the presence of resilience is a major protective factor for overcoming suicidal ideation and includes these five pillars: self-awareness, mindfulness, self-care, positive relationships, and purpose. The healing exercises in this book focus on helping you build these five pillars as a means to overcoming suicidal ideation and heal some of the pain that initially caused it.

My Heavy Coat of Trauma

I believe my ideation started due to my childhood trauma—which took me a while to identify. It wasn't until I was committed to working on myself regularly and getting help where all the wounding was exposed that I could start to unravel and deal with each issue during **Phase 1: Realization** of healing that we explore in Part 2. As I now dissect my suicidal episodes, I realize that I had a process and a pattern, and once the episode began, it was easy to step into the negative dialogue that played on a loop. I liken it to wearing a worn-out coat that was initially meant to keep me warm and safe but grew heavy and embedded with thorns. I'd put the coat on and let it take me down for days or weeks until something would break the energy. My childhood trauma created the narrative, "I am not worthy of being here. What I feel doesn't matter. I want to disappear. I will never have the life I crave." Trauma smothered the real me that I longed to share with the world.

As I reflect on my childhood, neglect was a present companion. The pain of the physical abuse pales compared to the duration and frequency at which I was left utterly alone. I remember thinking, "Why doesn't anyone want to be with me, play with me, hug me, read to me, swim with me, sleep with me, or hold me?" I feared the dark and had to sleep with all the lights on. I created a makeshift, tiny, self-sufficient room in my closet. When I got scared, this was where I felt the safest. I had a bed with pillows, a little TV, a cassette player with several tapes, my brown bear, and an ice pick I stole from the kitchen for protection. I would grab my dog Satchmo and stay there for hours, even through the night. I did this for most of my early childhood. My loneliness felt like a heavy weight on my chest. My mother worked until the bars closed, and my father was a car salesman who stayed out long past when his shift ended. My brother was only 5 years old when he was given the responsibility of me; neither of us received the care we deserved. Invisibility and abandonment created the foundation for my later suicidal ideation.

Clinging to the heavy trauma coat was a part of the false narrative I sold myself. I was deceived into thinking that this is how the world saw me. I found at times I would erroneously believe, "This is me forever; I am damaged goods." It was hard to imagine that I could have a totally different life when I was in ideation obsession. My trauma became a uniform I put on whenever a challenging life event would happen—impacting my energy, relationships, and experiences. The grim fact is that this energy of brokenness attracts more abuse, trauma, and thus suicidal ideation or self-destructive behavior.

Despite the pain and the false narratives, I continued to work on myself and hope for complete transformation and healing, but I didn't have any guarantees. I believed I could get to a healthy enough place where I could be aware of my thoughts and emotions enough to alert others when I needed help. I was committed to learning practices, modalities, or kinds of therapy to help me move forward. I was determined to surround myself with enough peace and love to get me through to the next day so that I could try again. I would say, "Just give it one more day and see how you feel tomorrow." This was my saving grace many times.❦

The goal of rebirth is for us to develop a new inner self and therefore a new soul, or spirit, but our inner self cannot be remade or reborn unless our outer self is too. Although we are spirits after death, we take with us into the other life aspects of our outer self: earthly emotions, doctrines, facts—in short, all the contents of our outer, earthly memory. These form the foundation on which our inner depths rest. Whatever priorities determine their arrangement, then, those are the priorities that inner things take on

 ## Trauma Bonds and Suicide

No one is completely immune to the risks of a trauma bond because the tactics used to create these bonds are manipulative and pervasive. Some risk factors do exist, however, that increase the likelihood of these bonds forming, and it may not be what you think. Those who are empathic, highly sensitive, intuitive, forgiving, and deeply caring are highly appealing to the efforts of a potential emotional abuser. This is why a positive relationship with oneself, where you truly know what your wants and needs are, is crucial in preventing a trauma bond from developing.

A common belief expressed by those with suicidal thoughts is of being a burden to others or experiencing guilt for needing support from those they love. These unhealthy beliefs serve as a risk factor for suicidality in trauma bonding because, in these types of bonds, there is a propensity to become overly dependent on one unhealthy relationship or person. The result is often the alienation of other supportive relationships, as well as a distorted sense of self and belief that the support system you once had is no longer willing to help. This negative narrative becomes even more detrimental when issues arise inside the trauma bond, further eroding self-esteem and self-worth. Self-worth is commonly tied to the desire to live or not, and if the person you are closest to is not supporting you, it may seem like the rest of the world will do the same. ☙

My Trauma Bonds

Because I didn't learn healthy boundaries in my family, I learned them through trial and error. Early on, I put loose limitations on what I would endure, and I would often start relationships with people who also came from trauma. Those people could direct me, in a sense, by gaslighting, or other forms of manipulation that likely stemmed from their own traumas and childhoods. We didn't talk much about gaslighting back then, but a person who employs this tactic could easily send me astray; I was malleable. I went from being that feisty, angry teenager to a fearful person with abandonment worries. I held my words instead of speaking my mind. Many of my early relationships were like this, but one stands out most vividly in my memory.

I will refer to this ex-partner as Steve. Something in me knew after our first date that I should never see him again. He kept pushing to be intimate, even when I explicitly said no. He pursued me heavily and quickly moved into my home—taking over my life and future. He was a hyper-controlling manipulator, and he broke me down rather quickly. He had a strong personality, and even other men were afraid of him. We stayed in a partnership three years beyond the expiration date. Eventually, all the intimacy had gone, along with the trust and most of the laughter. At that point, it seemed the fear of abandonment and being alone held us together. We would say, "Love you" when we ended calls, but we didn't feel it. I ignored it when he talked to other girls online. He was never physically abusive, but he was enormous, and I was smart enough not to cross him. I knew eventually things would end, and I would have to be strong. I had a feeling he was thinking the same thing. Something always stopped me from initiating the hard conversation—I couldn't do it.

I leaned back into my healing and spiritual communities. I kept my calendar full, going from yoga to meditation to clairvoyant energy training. This naturally brought in new, healthier relationships with people who had similar interests. Because my life was an empty glass, I filled it with positive people, things, and activities.

I reached out to my knowledgeable therapist, who helped me find the words and courage to end the relationship. I will refer to him as Dr. Stirling. His sessions were so profound that it's hard to imagine how he does that for every person, but I know he does. A passionate therapist can change your life. Many are modern-day heroes. He never got mad when I was dumping my pain onto him; he understood and invited my expression. I will share more about Dr. Stirling and our work in future chapters.

Through all these efforts, I was able to sever the last threads keeping Steve and I together. I felt the words that I had longed to say to him come from deep in my belly, up and out of my mouth. He moved out swiftly, and I was so relieved that I didn't even shed a tear. I had regained my sovereignty, my home, and my dignity. The trauma bond was broken, and it served both of us.

I don't carry any shame for being in this situation. Without Dr. Stirling explaining them to me in detail, I would not have known. To me it felt like we were glued together in a swamp, neither of us having the strength to pull us to freedom. With distance between us, I was able to see the clearer path and recognize that no matter what happened, I would make it. Being on my own would be much better than staying in something unhealthy since Steve was not the right partner for me. Survivors of abuse can easily be attracted to narcissists and gaslighters, so we must remain vigilant of who we let into our space, especially if we are the type that likes to heal, care, or over-give. ♥

Am I in a Trauma Bond?[17]

For the following exercise, take a moment to reflect on a relationship where your primary connection (past or present) seemed to be built on toxicity or an abuse cycle. Being compassionate with yourself and remaining curious and exploratory, answer "yes" or "no" for each of the following:

> Do you feel a strong emotional attachment to someone who has hurt or mistreated you?
>
> Do you make excuses for the person's behavior or minimize the abuse?
>
> Do you feel a sense of fear or anxiety when you think about leaving the person or the situation?
>
> Do you feel a sense of hopelessness or helplessness in relation to the person or the situation?
>
> Do you feel a sense of shame or guilt about the abuse or the relationship?
>
> Do you feel like you are "walking on eggshells" around the person to avoid conflict or abuse?
>
> Do you feel like you have lost touch with your own needs and desires in relation to the person or the situation?
>
> Do you feel like you have lost touch with your own sense of identity in relation to the person or the situation?
>
> Do you feel like you have lost touch with your own sense of self-worth in relation to the person or the situation?

If you answered "yes" to four or more questions, it may be indicative of a trauma bond. It is important to note that this is not a substitute for a professional evaluation by a licensed therapist or counselor. They will be able to provide more in-depth assessment and support to

17. Amelia Kelley, "Signs of a Toxic Relationship: Are You in a Trauma Bond?" Amelia Kelley, January 18, 2023, https://www.ameliakelley.com/quiz/signs-of-a-toxic-relationship-are-you-in-a-trauma-bond/.

help you process and overcome the potential trauma bond. It's also important to note that trauma bonding is a complex phenomenon, and it is not always easy to identify, and professional help is always recommended.

Knowing you are in a trauma bond is the first step; understanding how to extricate yourself from that relationship is the next. It is incredibly difficult to leave a toxic relationship, whether romantic, a friendship, family, or otherwise, as the trauma bond almost always involves moments of peace and repair. Try to remember what happens in the times when things are not healthy by checking in with a trusted person or perhaps journaling about these instances as they occur.

Addiction and Depression

Substance use is another one of the greatest risk factors for suicide. One of the main issues to consider with substance use is that it alters the brain chemistry responsible for the healthy production of neurotransmitters that improve mood and the ability to engage in effective decision making. Those with alcohol dependence are also ten times more likely than the general population to commit suicide, while those who use other illicit drugs are fourteen times more likely.[18] The risk of death becomes even higher with opioid use due to the rate of overdose and the difficulty in determining whether it was accidental or the result of a suicide attempt. Another factor that makes substance use more likely to lead to suicide is the presence of depression, which has long been believed to be the leading cause of and correlation to suicidal thoughts and attempts.

Depression on its own can lead to a loss of interest in things you once loved to do, which is known as anhedonia. This can include hopelessness, helplessness, isolation, physical pain, sleep disturbance, and a negative sense of self. When combining these issues with alcohol, which itself is a depressant, as well as an inhibitor for decision making, the combination further increases the risk of suicide.

18. Mina M. Rizk, Sarah Herzog, Sanjana Dugad, and Barbara Stanley, "Suicide Risk and Addiction: The Impact of Alcohol and Opioid Use Disorders," *Current Addiction Reports* 8 (2021): 194–207.

As you work to overcome suicidal thoughts, we want to encourage self-discovery and awareness. To do this, we have provided a brief checklist to help you reflect on your current substance use. Taking the time to be honest with yourself may help shed light on an issue before it causes further harm. If, after completing this list, you believe you may be struggling with addiction, we encourage you to reach out to a support group.

> *Angels constantly defend us and deflect the evil that the evil spirits intend against us. They even defend the falsity and evil we have in us, because they know very well where we obtained the falsity and evil: from evil spirits and demons. We never produce anything misguided or wicked out of ourselves. It is the evil spirits with us who produce it and at the same time cause us to believe that it comes from us. Such is their malevolence. What is more, at the same instant that they are filling us with these things and making us believe this way, they are also accusing and condemning us. —Emanuel Swedenborg, Secrets of Heaven 761*

Brief Substance Use Checklist

The following checklist measures the degree (mild, moderate, or severe) to which an individual meets the diagnostic criteria for a substance use disorder according to the *Diagnostic and Statistical Manual of Mental Disorders, Fifth Edition.*[19]

This screener is not intended to replace medical advice or diagnosis but may provide insight into whether further assessment or support may be beneficial to your journey of recovery from suicidal ideation.

The following statements are about your alcohol or drug use over the *past twelve months*. Please check YES for those statements that

---

19. American Psychiatric Association, *Substance-Related and Addictive Disorders.* In Diagnostic and Statistical Manual of Mental Disorders: DSM-5 (Washington, DC: American Psychiatric Association, 2013) https://doi.org/10.1176/appi.books.9780890425596, 490.

describe your drinking or drug use during the past twelve months and check NO for those statements that are not true for you.

		YES	NO
1	In the past 12 months, I often used alcohol or drugs in large amounts over longer periods of time than I intended.		
2	In the past 12 months, I often wanted or tried to cut down or control my alcohol or drug use.		
3	In the past 12 months, I spent a lot of time either (a) using alcohol or drugs, (b) in activities trying to obtain alcohol or drugs, or (c) recovering from the effects of my drinking or drug use.		
4	In the past 12 months, I gave up or reduced my involvement in important social, occupational, or recreational activities because of my alcohol or drug use.		
5	In the past 12 months, I continued to use alcohol or drugs despite knowing that it likely caused or made psychological or physical problems I had worse (for example, I continued drinking or drug use knowing it was making my ulcer or depression worse).		
6	In the past 12 months, I found I needed greater amounts of alcohol or drugs than I used to in order to feel intoxicated or to get a desired effect, OR I got much less of an effect by using the same amount of alcohol or drugs as in the past.		
7	In the past 12 months, I experienced withdrawal symptoms when I tried to cut down on or stop my drinking or drug use, OR I drank alcohol or used drugs to relieve or avoid withdrawal symptoms. **If Yes, please describe your withdrawal symptoms:** _____ _____		
8	In the past 12 months, my continued alcohol or drug use resulted in my not fulfilling major obligations at work, school, or home (for example, repeated absences or poor performances at work or school; neglecting my children or homelife).		
9	In the past 12 months, I repeatedly used alcohol or drugs in situations that were physically hazardous (e.g., driving a car or operating machinery).		

		YES	NO
10	In the past 12 months, I have experienced strong desires, urges, or cravings to use alcohol or drugs.		
11	In the past 12 months, I continued to use alcohol or drugs despite having persistent or recurrent social or interpersonal problems caused or made worse by the effects of my drinking or drug use (e.g., arguments with friends or family about my drinking or drug use or physical fights).		

Severity Coding:
> Mild: 2–3 symptoms
> Moderate: 4–5 symptoms
> Severe: 6 or more symptoms

Upon reviewing your results, take a moment to connect with self-compassion for where you are in your journey. If you uncover a potential substance use issue, it is beneficial to seek the support you deserve, as it truly could save your life. Reflection is best done in a nonjudgmental, loving way, with care and curiosity—the way you may approach an injured animal or beloved friend. It is common to experience levels of shame around this issue, and the more you can draw from self-love, as we explored in Chapter 1, the more likely you will receive the support you need to move forward on your healing journey.

If you do not meet the criteria for substance abuse, it is still help-ful to recognize that any time you mix substances such as alcohol or other illicit drugs with depression, anxiety, or despair, you increase the chance of engaging in self-harming behaviors or thoughts.

A Traumatized Child Builds an Unstable Future
As mentioned earlier, I moved away from my home at the age of four-teen, renting a room from my best friend's older sister in Scottsdale, Arizona. I started to thrive because all I had was me, and I trusted myself. I left school to work two jobs. I lied about my age, telling

employers I was eighteen. One day, an ex-schoolmate walked into the pizza shop and outed me: "Hey, how can you work here? You're only fourteen." But my rent was cheap, and I could always find more work. I had an edge, a rebellious spirit that sometimes left me feeling disconnected, ungrounded, and without boundaries. I hitchhiked alone in the desert, knowing it was dangerous. I put little value on myself and my life. The suicidal thinking I had from childhood had shifted into anger, and although I was actively not suicidal, my actions were self-destructive. The anger inside of me didn't go away like I expected it to when I was no longer living in that loveless and abusive home. I didn't want to die, but I cared little if I existed. I believe part of what saved me was that I was so sensitive to alcohol and drugs, that I never got into a cycle of abusing them. I know how trauma and addiction directly connect with each other, and luck was on my side that I did not go down that path.

In 1987, when I finally turned seventeen, I jumped into my Ford Ranger and left Arizona and its majestic mountains for sunny Los Angeles, my birthplace. I had no connections there, but I'd heard a lot about this place called the "Sunset Strip" and the creative people who gathered there. It didn't take long for me to feel a sense of belonging. I joined creative circles of writers, musicians, filmmakers, and entrepreneurs, most of whom were fellow trauma-wounded misfits, many of whom I still know to this day. News traveled fast within my social circles about date rapes by GHB-spiked drinks, stalkers, and various threats. We had to be vigilant and watch each other's backs.

My social lifestyle conflicted with my fierce desire to succeed in life. I wanted to prove to everyone that I was worthy. I took a job at an insurance company. Living on little money, and in my car at times, I had to get donations for clothes and food from people at work. I was trying to survive on my own in this all-too-real world. The chaos of actual survival temporarily took my mind off suicidal ideation.

I yearned for a safer life and focused on changing my circumstances. Signing up with a temp agency that placed me at the Walt Disney Studios during the day, I finally had a job with benefits. I was a fast learner and hard worker and had a great work ethic. With this position, as well as a hostess job at a restaurant at night, I was able to get my first one-bedroom apartment on Ventura Boulevard. I was 19 years old. I got a Persian cat named Scotch. I remember being very proud of myself—decorating the house with thrift-store finds. I registered at Glendale Community College and started taking UCLA film and television classes. I recall it being a good time in my life; my youth was not being wasted. The suitors appeared from all angles, and I was in a few relationships but nothing that made my heart sing. I did a little modeling on the side, and one of the agents offered me a job, and then suddenly, I was working as an agent. They said I had an incredible eye for pleasing facial compositions, something I think inspires my artwork today. I got bored answering to my boss at the time, who was an abusive drug addict, and I saw an opportunity to make money and started my own modeling agency, Cavalier Models. I rented the space right above the Whiskey a Go-Go on Sunset Boulevard. With the success of the modeling agency, I was able to buy my first home in the San Fernando Valley when I was only 23 years old. During this timeframe, my world was my career, but just beneath the surface were wounds that would come out soon enough. I pitched an idea for a radio show on KIEV 870 AM and ended up a producer. There, I met the man who would become my husband

It was 1993. He was a fiery, red-haired, freckled poet and musician, native to Dublin, Ireland, and ten years my senior. He had already been in a well-known UK band but was out on his own in California, forming a new band. He invited me to see him perform at a local pub named Molly Malones. I became a regular at his shows. I mustered the courage to ask him out for a drink, and he replied confidently that if I opened up to his charm, he would stake his claim over me. He was right. He moved in within months, and we fell in love.

Our fast-paced romance quickly led to marriage and promises of forever. We spent the early part of our marriage happy, sitting on our porch as he sang to me, wrote songs, gained a record deal, and planned our future children. He toured a lot, which was hard on us because we both hated being alone, kicking up both of our histories of abandonment and neglect. I craved security and sought it from him, though I should have been looking inward and working on myself. I know now that a secure union is made of two individuals who are strong in themselves first and foremost.

He wrote his first four albums with me, and he would sit at his desk with his guitar in his lap and his head on his hand, painstakingly playing with lyrics. He would hide little words in there because he didn't want his fans to think he wrote overt love songs. When he was done, he played it for me, pointing out the secret meanings for our love story. I believed I was a part of his creative expressions. We would sing and dance and duet to songs like, The Pogues' "Fairytale of New York." We would go to thrift stores and buy fancy outfits to attend the theater, symphony, and opera. He introduced me to his favorite composers and writers like Beethoven, Oscar Wilde, George Bernard Shaw, and James Joyce. I listened to everything he said, a sponge craving to be taught. We used to fall asleep holding each other so tight, waking up holding hands, like we were afraid to let go. He would draw me cartoons and leave them around the house, saying, "I let an angel clips my wings."

Did I mention he was from Ireland? He was a drinker. There was the "wine guy, whiskey guy, and beer guy," and he acted differently depending on his beverage. He would get either lovey-dovey or nasty when he drank. One evening, we were drinking and "whiskey guy" was in attendance, and I shared my insecurity and sadness about him being gone so much. He was averaging nine months of touring out of the year. That night he got nasty—saying, "You're not book smart; you're stupid." He knew my weak spot was my cobbled education and learning disabilities. I had a past pile of "I'm sorry" letters from him because he would always apologize the next day. That night turned into a bigger fight. My identity was wrapped up in being his wife, having kids, and building our life; but I feared he would leave me, even though I knew he loved me. In his drunken stupor, he attacked my most vulnerable self, shouting, "I am going to leave you!"

I felt numb.

This was the first time that he had ever said anything like this so I wholeheartedly believed that he would be gone in the morning. My heart raced, tears poured out of my eyes, my head throbbed, and I could feel blood rushing to my face. I swear I could hear my heart breaking, my soul torn out of my body so far away that I couldn't find it anymore. I was tired of crying, of being in fear, being alone, not good enough, or strong enough. I couldn't bear seeing the person I loved leave me, so I told myself there was no way out but to exit this place. If I left, I wouldn't have to climb that mountain of pain.

He continued to shout at me. He made fun of me for not knowing where I wanted to take my career. "Why can't you be more like me? I've known my whole life I wanted to be a singer. You have nothing to offer this world!"

I decided he was right. I didn't deserve to be here. I took a beat. I went quiet. If I left, I wouldn't have to hear any more words that hurt. I was in what we detail as **Phase 5: Action,** which we outline in Chapter 3. I looked blankly in his red eyes as his thick Irish brogue spat wild things. When I decided what I was going to do, my whole body went cold. I walked over to the knife drawer and pulled out the first knife I could see. I grabbed the handle with all my pain and energy and swiped it horizontally across my wrist.

Blood poured out fast. I dropped the knife and grabbed the cut with my hand. I was shocked how deep it was. He grabbed my wrist too and asked me what I had done; he was instantly in helper mode. He ran to the first aid kit, got gauze and medical tape, and bandaged my arm. I felt instant regret and embarrassment. It was very late at night, but I called my primary doctor, and he met me a few hours later at his office.

The look on my doctor's face was one of total sadness and frustration. He would not let my husband in the room as he stitched me up quietly. He had known me for years and helped me through some difficult times when I did not have family to support me. He said he was not sure my husband deserved my loyalty and kindness. I promised him I would never do it again.

The after-attempt feelings were much worse. The embarrassment endured for not just days but months. My mind was shouting at me, "You are such a loser!" I pretended to be okay because I didn't want to look crazy but inside, this act made me want to do it even more. My wrist still looks like Sally from *Nightmare Before Christmas,* white stitch markings on the skin.

In his band, there were seven band members; one a female. She put restrictions on wives touring and even though they were gone all of the time, I only joined him once. This woman created situations where he would have to choose between me and the band, intentionally separating us. We could both see what she was doing and at one point he even auditioned to replace her, but I felt a shift in him. The energy and love he had always given to me was no longer there. One night they called me from a hotel room in Germany and told me that they were best friends. They were so drunk he didn't even remember the call. This was not the right life for me. I knew it but I didn't want to let him go.

One night just after our fifth anniversary, I pulled in from work and stopped in the driveway. Something was different. He was at the sink doing dishes. I put my bags down, and he turned to me and said he was leaving me. I lost the use of my knees and fell to the ground. I wanted death to come at that moment. He sat with me and cried too.

"Gina, I am doing this for you."

How could this be for me?

But he knew that I deserved better because he was not going to be home, and he was not interested in spirituality.

He left me in 2003, which led to the worst suicidal ideation I ever experienced. I would lay in our bed, sometimes for days, and look at the tree that he'd proposed to me under and imagine my body hanging there. I would walk over to it and throw a rope over and test it, and look for a stool. I imagined how I would look with a broken neck and worried, what if I missed?

I didn't tell anyone how I was feeling—not even my husband, when he would call and check on me.

I now understand that if this had not happened, I would not have evolved into the person I am today. It sent me on a journey to heal myself, to look for angels and guides like Emanuel Swedenborg to lift me up and support me. ♥

> *We are all born human, which means that we have the image of God within us. The image of God within us is our ability to discern what is true and to do what is good. Our ability to discern what is true comes from divine wisdom and our ability to do what is good comes from divine love. This ability is the image of God; it is enduring with everyone who is whole and is never erased.* —*Emanuel Swedenborg*, Divine Providence 322

Poverty and Medical Illness

Another risk factor for suicide is poverty, especially when coupled with medical illness. The deprivation, debt, and inequality caused by economic instability can either exacerbate suicidal thoughts or potentially initiate them. This becomes even more detrimental when there are chronic medical illnesses involved, as the ability to work and support oneself is often impacted. Recent news focusing on misused right-to-die laws in Canada have shown that the country's struggling medical system is forcing those with chronic illness to contemplate ending their lives, even if what they prefer is financial assistance and a beacon of hope. When your medical bills are more than your assistance checks, you drown, especially if you cannot work and you are in a constant state of pain. This can all become a form of chronic trauma that impacts your desire to live in this world. In an article in *The Guardian*,[20] a 51-year-old Ontario woman known as Sophia was granted physician-assisted death after her chronic condition became

20. Leyland Cecco, "Are Canadians Being Driven to Assisted Suicide by Poverty or Healthcare Crisis?" *The Guardian*, May 11, 2022.

intolerable and her meager disability stipend left her little to survive on. According to CTV News,[21] she shared: "The government sees me as expendable trash, a complainer, useless and a pain in the ass." For two years, she and friends had pleaded without success for better living conditions.

We must find a better way to support those who are not economically secure. Approximately 75 percent of suicides in the world occur in low- and middle-income countries where rates of poverty are high. This is inexcusable, as all human life deserves security. What we can do is bring further attention to this issue by carrying out necessary research and highlighting the appropriate policy changes that must be made to protect humankind.

Men and Suicide

When speaking about risk, it is important to recognize how suicidality presents in men. In the United States, men die by suicide at rates four times greater than women, and their deaths account for upward of 75 to 80 percent of suicides in total, with roughly 105 men dying by suicide every day. Being single, being financially unstable, or having a troubled childhood further increase the risk of suicide for men—likely due to heteronormative expectations about masculinity.

We must begin addressing these issues by normalizing the conversations around suicide, especially with young boys and men. There is a misunderstanding that suicidal thoughts are abnormal or a sign of emotional or mental weakness—it is quite the contrary. Research shows that lifetime prevalence of suicidal ideation is at least twelve percent for all genders, which accounts for nearly four hundred thousand people in the United States alone. Suicidal thoughts are by no means uncommon, nor should they be labeled as such. We choose to have difficult conversations with our children around topics such as

21. Avis Favaro, "Woman with Chemical Sensitivities Chose Medically-Assisted Death After Failed Bid to Get Better Housing," *CTV News*, Updated August 24, 2022, https://www.ctvnews.ca/health/woman-with-chemical-sensitivities-chose-medically-assisted-death-after-failed-bid-to-get-better-housing-1.5860579.

sex, or drug and alcohol abuse, because avoiding these topics does not make it less likely they will occur. We should be doing the same with the topic of suicide, as having open and honest conversations with young boys and men about their mental health is proactive and makes it more likely we can prevent potentially tragic endings.

The cultural pressure on young boys and men to repress their emotions in fear of not seeming "man enough" is another detrimental component to the epidemic of suicide for this group. Research has shown that masculinity norms such as being self-reliant and not needing to ask for help put men at greater risk of experiencing suicidal thoughts.

As a society, we need to encourage young boys and men to break out of harmful stereotypes around what it means to be a man and know that asking for support is purely human. Men's experiences with suicidal thoughts are often shrouded in stigma that keeps all of us from talking about the issue, but this needs to change. Some strides are being made, such as books like *Man Enough* by Justin Baldoni,[22] as well as the affiliated podcast by the same name or The ManKind Initiative documentary *Real Men Do Cry,* which explores the physical and mental effects of domestic abuse on men.[23]

Preconceived notions about masculinity, such as thinking men should be strong and stoic protectors and providers, put incredible pressure on men to disconnect from their feelings and potential sensitivities. Being a "man" does not equate with being emotionless, and if we continue to see men in this way, we are also encouraging instances of aggression, violence, and unresolved anger.

It is up to each of us to ask the men in our lives how they are doing, what they are feeling, and what they need. The adage "man up" has no place in suicide prevention. If, instead, we can view the willingness to express and be vulnerable as an act of courage on the part of men,

22. Justin Baldoni. *Man Enough: Undefining My Masculinity* (HarperCollins, 2021).
23. The ManKind Initiative, "Real Men Do Cry," YouTube, August 17, 2016, https://www.youtube.com/watch?v=PbjBc9CipBg.

we will be that much closer to reducing the chance that our brothers, sons, husbands, fathers, and friends die by suicide.

| The adage "man up" has no place in suicide prevention. |

Soldier Suicide

Our armed forces face a particular risk of suicide. A 2021 study found that 30,177 active-duty personnel and veterans, who served in the military after the September 11th, 2001 attacks, have died by suicide since, as compared to the 7,057 service members killed in combat in those same twenty years. The Military Suicide Awareness #22ADAY Movement has created a call to action, shedding light on the average of twenty-two veterans who die by suicide each day. According to the US Department of Veteran Affairs[24] rates continue to climb and are currently at an all-time high of 1.66 times greater in the veteran population versus the civilian population. It is more important than ever that we as a nation devise a plan to intervene, support, and save the people who have sacrificed so much for our country.

When discussing this issue with veterans in my therapy practice, the resounding message is that they are not receiving the mental health support they require and are desperately seeking. In the *New York Times* article, "A Secret War, Strange New Wounds, and Silence From the Pentagon,"[25] writer Dave Phillips recounted stories from a collection of soldiers who returned from deployment with mysterious and "life-shattering" mental health issues leading to psychosis, hallucinations, and suicidal and homicidal ideation—despite many of them being miles from the front lines. Not directly witnessing trauma or combat meant that when these soldiers took the PTSD and traumatic brain injury (TBI) screeners required to receive services upon their

24. Brenda Mooney, "Despite Expanded Efforts by VA, Veteran Suicides Rose Slightly in Recent Report," *U.S. Medicine*, 2023, https://www.usmedicine.com/block/despite-expanded-efforts-by-va-veteran-suicides-rose-slightly-in-recent-report/.
25. Dave Phillips, "A Secret War, Strange New Wounds, and Silence from the Pentagon," *New York Times*, Updated March 15, 2024, https://www.nytimes.com/2023/11/05/us/us-army-marines-artillery-isis-pentagon.html.

return, the scales often did not capture the underlying issues they were returning home with. The screeners were not accounting for the chronic, yet normalized, stress experienced by these soldiers along with the impact traumatic brain injuries have on suicidality.

The origins of the brain injuries incurred by the soldiers in the more recent wars were deemed a mystery until recent findings about the strategic approach the United States took to fight the Islamic State. According to the *New York Times* article, the strategy was to dramatically reduce soldiers deployed, intended to save lives by employing air strikes, as well as smaller groups on the ground firing tens of thousands of high-explosive shells—far more than any American artillery battery has fired since the Vietnam War. While soldiers' lives were in fact saved, the death and devastation came when they returned home with mental and physical health problems connected to the traumatic brain injuries they had suffered. Research revealed a 1.9 ratio increase in suicides in those with TBI resulting from the impact of detonation versus those without. Symptoms including increased levels of impulsivity and reduced ability to perceive long-term perspectives and consequences, as well as increased instances of depression and potential isolation and perceived helplessness were attributed to an increased risk of suicide.

To save the lives of our veterans and improve outcomes for their mental health, the military must shift toward a resilience model. Veterans I work with often express frustration at not being given the time and space to grieve what they experience both while deployed and during the rigors of enlistment. In his book, *My Grandmother's Hands: Racialized Trauma and the Pathway to Mending Our Hearts and Bodies*,[26] Resmaa Menakem explores how a similar culture exists in law enforcement, where officers who encounter trauma on the job are not provided time and space to process what their bodies and minds experience.

---

26. Resmaa Menakem, *My Grandmother's Hands: Racialized Trauma and the Pathway to Mending Our Hearts and Bodies,* Las Vegas, NV: Central Recovery Press, 2017.

There are, of course, reasons for this mentality in such spaces like the military and law enforcement. As Richard Doss puts it in his TedX Naperville Talk, *Trained Not to Cry: The Challenge of Being a Soldier,*[27] his drill sergeant once said, "I cannot teach you two things at the same time. Either I am teaching you to be hard or I am teaching you to be soft." When it comes to standing up to life-or-death scenarios, there is validity to this statement, but what about aftercare? What if after the trauma there is a normalization to talk, counsel, support, not minimize, not placate or make fun of emotions, and, when possible, rest? How might our veterans reintegrate into civilian life if these resilience practices, which we will explore at length in this book, were part of the training offered to the military to keep the mental and physical health of these soldiers strong? Better yet would be if those in leadership roles adopted these practices and encouraged the culture themselves; what if we held them accountable for the casualties by suicide that occur under their watch? The hope would be that soldiers become more likely to participate in the resources that are currently available, such as mental health counseling and treatment offered by the VA, to enhance skills needed to perform their duty as opposed to it being seen as a sign of weakness or shame. Shifting focus to a resilience model in the military would also make it more likely that discharged veterans would seek out support to smooth the transition back to civilian life.

When considering reintegration to society, research shows that the most vulnerable time for veterans occurs after discharge when they struggle to readjust to civilian life and acquire the social support they need. Building a community with other veterans, finding a purpose or mission such as going back to school or finding employment, connecting with other civilian communities, and/or finding a religion or spiritual practice that supports the transition are all helpful protective factors.

27. Richard Doss, "Trained Not to Cry: The Challenge of Being a Soldier," YouTube Video, July 21, 2023, https://youtube.com/watch?v=WkCq6BWFBAM.

Another area of focus that is lacking in preventing suicide is researching effective treatments for TBI with brain-based treatments such as transcranial magnetic stimulation (TMS), a procedure that uses magnetic fields to stimulate nerve cells in the brain to improve symptoms of depression. TMS has been used in practice since 1985 but only acquired FDA approval as of 2008. This treatment is a powerful option for improving symptoms of depression that can lead to suicidality, and further research into its use for TBI is being conducted. It took nearly twenty years of research to acquire FDA approval; TMS is now readily available to those with health insurance.

Neurofeedback is biofeedback that teaches self-control over brain functions by measuring brain waves and providing a feedback signal, normally involving viewing a television screen while brain waves are measured. This intervention is showing incredible promise, but the research has not been funded at a rate robust enough to bring this potentially life-saving treatment to those who need it. I can personally attest to its power as I have seen it support the recovery of both my clients and even one of my closest family members. I quite literally witnessed the unveiling of my loved one's ability to think, feel, and engage in life after completing treatment, and I believe it saved their life.

With regard to all of the risk factors we have explored, change can be slow, and when you are personally experiencing these forms of trauma, poverty, or chronic illness, it can be difficult to handle the distress. The following skill provides a technique to help manage these feelings and care for yourself at this very moment.

EMDR Spiral Skill Meditation for Distress

Part of healing and overcoming suicidal ideation is processing past trauma, mental illness, and unhealthy relationships, which can lead to overwhelming emotions that may increase suicidal thoughts and ideation. This chapter itself may have brought some of these feelings up; reading about the risk factors associated with suicidal ideation may have triggered what has been especially difficult about your experiences. To help alleviate these intense emotions, we want to offer a way to be with these sensations without avoiding or dissociating (numbing and feeling disconnected from oneself). While dissociation is sometimes necessary for survival, it can also hinder growth and the ability to feel fully alive. To offer a way to cope with any difficult feelings that may have arisen from reading the content in this chapter, we would like to offer an exercise derived from a gold-standard treatment of trauma called EMDR (eye movement desensitization and reprocessing). Created by Francine Shapiro,[28] EMDR offers a highly accessible, self-directed meditation called the EMDR Spiral Technique that provides a safe way to bring presence to and process uncomfortable feelings—all while reducing suicidal ideation. One way you can use this skill specifically to reduce suicidal thoughts is to find those thoughts in your body and follow all eight steps with that as your target.

The EMDR Spiral Technique

1. Bring to mind a memory or experience that you find mildly disturbing (this skill can be used for intense cognitions, as well, if you are safe).

2. Rate this memory or event on a 0-to-10 scale (otherwise known as Subjective Units of Distress (SUD), which we will use through the book): 0 means you can remain completely calm, whereas 10 is maximum activation.

3. Notice where you are feeling the most disturbance in your body by noticing which parts begin to feel tense, tight, or uncomfortable.

4. Concentrate on that feeling and space in your body (for instance, tightness in your chest) and imagine that those sensations are a

---

28. Francine Shapiro, *Getting Past Your Past: Take Control of Your Life with Self-help Techniques from EMDR Therapy,* New York, NY: Rodale Press, 2013.

spiral moving in your body. Notice if the spiral moves clockwise or counterclockwise.

5. Allow your eyes (while closed) to gently follow the spiral up, down, and around in a circular motion.

6. Once you notice a change in sensation in your body, use your mind to change the direction of the spiral, noticing anything that happens.

7. Choose which direction felt most grounding for you and end by moving the spiral in that direction.

8. Write down anything you noticed or felt in the space below:

_____

_____

_____

There was a large crowd of spirits around me that sounded like a sort of chaotic stream. The spirits complained that everything was now going to ruin, because everything seemed disconnected among them, which made them fearful that the end was coming. They thought there would be total destruction, as is usual in these situations. In their midst, though, I picked up a sound that was gentle, angelic, and sweet, containing only what was orderly. Angelic choruses were on the inside, and the confused crowd of spirits was on the outside. The angelic flow lasted a long time. I was told that it represented the way the Lord works from what is peaceful within to control what is messy and uncontrolled on the outside. Through this core of peace he reduces the chaos on the outer bounds to order, rescuing each part from the error of its own nature. —Emanuel Swedenborg, Secrets of Heaven *5396a*

CONCLUSION: YOU DESERVE TO HEAL

While it can be difficult to explore how the heaviness of trauma, mental and physical illness, substance use, and poverty increase suicidality, we are choosing to leave nothing unexplored. To further understand how you can be impacted by suicidal thoughts, in the next chapter we will explain the **5 Phases of Suicidal Ideation.** Knowing that each person is unique, these phases serve as a blueprint for what is common for most people. As you reflect, allow time to recognize any similarities or differences between your and Gina's experiences of these phases.

Chapter 3: The Experience

The overarching rule for the spiritual world's influence on us is that we cannot think or will anything on our own; everything flows in. Goodness and truth come from the Lord through heaven and therefore through the angels with us. Evil and falsity come from hell and therefore through the evil spirits with us. Their influence is exerted on our thinking and our willing. —Emanuel Swedenborg, Secrets of Heaven 5846

SUICIDAL IDEATION IS progressive and occurs on a continuum with common phases for most people. Understanding these phases offers insight into warning signs, as well as useful language to describe your experience. Awareness is important not only for the person suffering suicidal thoughts but also for healers, helping professionals, family, and friends. We need to be talking directly to the person who is suicidal about their experience if we are ever going to help them remain safe. If you personally have experienced thoughts of suicide, or are experiencing them right now, you can use these phases to describe which one you find yourself in.

As you review the phases, remember it is *normal* to vacillate between them. Many people fluctuate in phases 1 and 2, so approaching this experience with compassion and curiosity is best. The emotions and experiences in these phases are part of the human condition and do not definitively mean someone will progress toward suicide, but rather, this is part of the potential range of coping in the face of suffering. These phases are a continuum of suicidal ideation meant to help you understand how negative thoughts can progress to self-harm or active planning for some individuals.

The **5 Phases of Suicidal Ideation** explored in this book begin with a cognitive shift in perspective and end with plans and attempts to take one's own life. The five phases are:

Phase 1: Contemplation

Phase 2: Hopelessness

Phase 3: Despair

Phase 4: Intent

Phase 5: Action

This chapter provides a detailed description of each of these phases, as well as Gina's personal reflections on how these phases manifested in her own life. At the end of each phase, there will be a section for you to journal about your own experience with each phase in the past or present. If there is a phase you have not experienced, you can journal your thoughts, concerns, or questions about the phase described. Knowing what questions you have can help you begin important conversations with your support system. ♥

The 5 Phases of Suicidal Ideation

 PHASE 1: CONTEMPLATION

This phase includes considering suicide as an option, leading to an internal shift toward its potential. The thought of suicide no longer feels distant or terrifying, but rather, something one could consider. There may be an increased interest in stories of those who have committed suicide, or the person may begin asking others what they think about it. At this point, the individual is not likely to discuss their own views on suicide with others unless the topic is readily addressed—another reason why normalizing the topic of suicide is a crucial measure for prevention.🫘

 A Thwarted Sense of Belonging

When I was in this phase, thoughts around the finality of suicide and the acts to get there were not yet front and center. My primary feeling was a deep sense of not belonging to the world, despite being close enough to witness everything. In this phase, I felt just outside of the circle at home, school, work, and in social groups. At times, I felt I didn't even belong to myself. I was moving and living in the world but not fully present inside, numb and grayed-out. I could stand in a crowd with a plastic smile on my face while a dark cloud hovered overhead, churning out thoughts like,

"I don't fit in."

"Do I have an eternal sign on my back that reads, 'Kick Hard Here'?"

"Nobody understands who I am and what I need."

"I am lonely."🫘

How has Phase 1 manifested in my life?

_____

_____

_____

 PHASE 2: HOPELESSNESS
At this phase, there is a preoccupation with the idea that whatever painful situation the person is experiencing will not get any better. This leads to a reduced fear of death that is not based on spiritualism nor on a connection with the afterlife. Instead, it is due to a decline in self-preservation, as well as in the natural desire to stay alive. In this phase, there may be an increase in imagining one's own death. At this point, the individual may share their thoughts about death and dying with others but will not necessarily reference suicide.

 Internal Bargaining
At this phase, the reduced fear of death became more present, and I was starting to feel even less connection with self-love. I was being self-destructive, and my self-esteem was suffering greatly. I noticed that instead of thinking of the consequences of what I was doing, I was instead acting impulsively. I also noticed that thoughts that were normal to others about the fear of losing their lives seemed less

alarming to me. Much like being in an airplane where the turbulence is rough: others are scared, while I perk up because it would be a welcomed thing if something were to happen.

All kinds of bargaining can happen at this phase, and it's different for everyone. The bargaining involves ways to improve life by getting that promotion, new job, or a new relationship. For example, we can deceive ourselves into thinking that achieving the physique we've always wanted will destroy the dark thoughts. Without deep emotional and mental healing, nothing changes, and it will become even more frustrating. Most of us realize we should let someone know what is happening to us, but the fear of judgment and damage to our relationships and professional status scares us more; so we stay quiet. ☕

How has Phase 2 manifested in my life?

_____

_____

_____

 PHASE 3: DESPAIR
The act of suicide becomes a viable consideration due to repeated suffering. This phase can sometimes feel like a pit of despair as options to change one's own life seem fleeting. Many trauma survivors and those with severe mental illness find themselves stuck in this phase for long periods of time (even years) unless they actively employ resilience tactics. When engaging in the skills presented in this book, it is quite possible to move back to earlier phases. At this phase, the individual is most likely to share their mental pain around suicide with trusted individuals such as therapists or close friends. This phase is also when individuals may share their emotional anguish and struggles with mental illness. All thoughts shared at this phase should be taken seriously and are not merely a cry for attention. It is unlikely that the individual will begin preparing for suicide, but there is an increased

sense of hopelessness about their mental or emotional health issues. The person's sleep routine or wellness habits may start to suffer as well during this phase.

 The Rabbit Hole

This is the phase where real suicidal ideation entered my thoughts. I experienced a low hum warning that any significant issue or unexpected life event could throw me down the rabbit hole.

I wanted the constant hum of this pain to stop. My emotional tank felt empty, while anxiety surged. I struggled to get to sleep and woke up groggy, intensifying my worries and obscuring clear thought. I made mistakes on projects and when my work was criticized, I took it to heart, feeling like the world was against me.

At this point, I was working in what I had long thought of as my dream job. My grandfather had also worked for this company in the 1930s and I felt like it was my birthright. I pursued every angle to get inside, but once there, the job was no dream. My boss was jealous of the attention I received in meetings because people assumed I was the superior. I formed an employee-run leadership group to bring people together, signing up 1,500 people in three months and a board with a waitlist. I produced events with record-breaking attendance, speaking to sold-out crowds of hundreds. The CEO began consulting me about new projects on the horizon. The more attention I got, the crueler my boss became. On her birthday, I gifted her a cool old journal from the seventies. She said coolly, "Oh dear, don't you know you are not supposed to gift up?" The whole room went quiet.

I had been in physical pain for three years and left on medical leave to have my back fused. When I returned, they let me go for poor performance. I felt that I was not treated fairly and initiated a lawsuit. It was very scary; they deposed me repeatedly, buried my lawyer in thousands of documents, followed me and my family, and combed through my trash in the middle of the night. I wanted to have a voice, but it left me balancing on a tight rope between staying and leaving this world. I ultimately couldn't take it.

Thoughts of suicide became my secret obsession. Out at a restaurant with friends, seemingly engaged, I imagined going home and saying goodbye to everyone and everything. I feared that any effort to heal would fail, and I would find only more disappointment. "This isn't going to change; why are you still here?"

In this phase, I isolated from and didn't engage in family and community activities. I made it seem like I was always working on something and simply too busy. I did tell one of my best friends about my suicidal thoughts. She responded, "I talked to my husband, and he says that I am not a doctor, and I can't help you and that you need professional help." My heart fell into my stomach because telling someone was the hardest thing I had ever done. It felt as though the door was slammed shut. While I don't blame her for setting boundaries—she was right—I now had double the fear of telling anyone.

It took me a long time to let Dr. Stirling know about my suicidality, which feels sad because I did trust him. I have learned now through my study of suicidality that many people do not disclose their suicidal thoughts to their therapists.[29] I feared he would have to make a call and I would wind up in a cloth coat with straps. I had bills to pay and things to do and no partner to pick up the pieces. I believe the stigma of suicidal ideation is why people hold off telling anyone.

---

29. David J. Hallford, "Most People Don't Disclose Their Suicidal Thoughts," *Psychology Today*, April 22, 2023, https://www.psychologytoday.com/us/blog/our-wonderful-messy-minds/202304/we-dont-talk-about-ending-our-lives.

If you are at this phase, please tell people you know immediately. If you don't have anyone, please reach out to one of the resources listed at the back of this book (page 212), tell them, and get help with making a safety plan.

It's important for me to state here that these situations have all been healed for me. I am presenting them so you might see that I understand hardship and relate to your pain. When you reach **Phase 5: Confidence** in the phases of healing, these memories will still be there but the negative charge with which they can activate you dissolves a little over time until they are gone. ♡

How has Phase 3 manifested in my life?

_____

_____

_____

> *It is evil spirits who stir up our falsities and evil. From our memory they stir up everything we have ever considered or committed since childhood. Evil spirits are able to do this with such consummate skill and malice that words cannot describe it. The angels who accompany us, though, bring out the goodness and truth that we have and use it to defend us. The conflict between the parties is what we sense and feel, and it causes our conscience to gnaw at us and torment us. —Emanuel Swedenborg,* Secrets of Heaven *751*

PHASE 4: INTENT
Thoughts and actions around suicide increase in the form of self-harm or dangerous actions. At this point, "suicidal-type behaviors" may increase (cutting, drunk driving, ignoring medical needs), and for some, there may be a spontaneous suicide attempt that does not include a plan. Safety is a major concern at this phase, as many individuals may

cause permanent physical damage with hasty self-harm attempts. At this phase, the individual will be more likely to share their mental pain and suicidal thoughts, mainly with trusted individuals such as therapists or close friends.☙

The Quicksand

When I learned about quicksand as a child, it terrified me to think that I could sink in the sand and just disappear. That visual stuck with me, and it seems the best image to match what Phase 4 felt like. While suicidal ideation is an internal experience and not something that grabs at you from the ground below, it is just as severe and can feel the same.

I was stuck between feeling disconnected and fearful, one step away from suicidal thoughts at all times. At this phase, I felt that if just one more difficult thing happened, I would be sucked into a dark place. The feelings of unworthiness and hopelessness were invasive and could no longer be laughed off, ignored, or quieted. I hoped that someone would rush in and hold me during these times. I wished for someone to encourage me to just give it one more day, to wait a little longer for a change of state to arrive. While I know this would have meant so much to me at this phase, I also know that, ultimately, we need to cultivate this loving voice inside ourselves.

This is the point where I felt my contemplation of suicide shift toward serious consideration. I spent a great deal of time crying softly, while harmful scenarios played in my head. More than anything, I wanted the suffering to stop, and I fantasized about the relief. An internal voice whispered that if I followed through on my suicidal thoughts, I wouldn't have to deal with the pain anymore, while another part of me knew if I could just get up and walk, I might feel better. Everything felt so heavy.

I remember driving to California from Arizona when I was stuck in this phase. It was nighttime and raining hard. I was in my truck, and I put my foot down on the gas pedal and sped through the rain, weaving around diesel trucks, stone cold in my mind and feeling disconnected. I knew I was putting myself in danger, and that was the point. It's hard to write this because I didn't consider I was putting others in danger too. For that, I am so sorry.

I can only say that a guardian angel was on my side that night, and I am eternally grateful I don't ever have to feel like that again, especially now that I have found spiritual tools that are available anywhere.

How has Phase 4 manifested in my life?

_____

_____

_____

 PHASE 5: ACTION

At this phase, the fear of death has been all but removed, and suicide seems like a viable option for ending suffering. The individual will become mentally focused on their plan and method for ending their life, leading them to seem less distressed and more at ease with their decision. The person will likely isolate, making less effort to engage in activities or relationships that were once important to them. Many will withdraw as they tie up loose ends, such as who will take their beloved pet, quitting a job, giving away their belongings, or finalizing their legal will. For many, this phase includes a detailed plan of action for suicide, and lethal attempts are made. At this phase, the individual will be unlikely to share their plan or intent to commit suicide unless they feel unconditionally supported or there is a specific intervention by a trusted person or professional.

The Tar Pit

The quicksand is one thing, but the tar pits of Phase 5 are another level. I descended down the rabbit hole, through the quicksand and landed in thick, sticky black tar. All my senses dulled. Being this depressed took a tremendous toll on my energy. It was like I convinced myself I had a terminal illness and I was going to unalive myself. Sometimes, I found myself thinking as if I had already committed suicide. In Phase 5, I felt like death was already upon me but the rebirth I desperately wanted was so far away. I would think, "It seems like a million miles away; I've already gone too far and can't turn back now."

I had always wanted a family, but my tubal pregnancies rendered me unable to have children. I tried many different friend and work circles, but felt I was only accepted when I was doing things that benefitted them.

At this stage, there was a definite difference. I accepted this as my life and doors closed, without me ever receiving the things I wanted to experience.

The chaos went calm. I formed the premeditated way I was going to say goodbye. I had accumulated at least half a million dollars in equity in my home. I planned to sell it, go high on the hog in a swanky place in the Hollywood Hills amongst the stars. I dreamed of a blowout final birthday party with a big band.

I thought if I gave away all my money that it would be another reason to leave and there was nothing holding me back. I gifted one of my friends $3,000 for sitting on the phone with me and letting me cry. I paid the legal fees of another friend, the vet bills of a third. I imagined all of the donations to charities I supported.

Amidst this pain, I had two lifelines that stopped me every time: my dogs and my mother. I wondered, "Who will take care of the rescue dogs I promised to care for?" or, "If I die, my mom will have lost both her children to death by their own means." I couldn't abandon my beloved companions or be the source of more pain for my mother.

As I think back now, it is heartbreaking to reflect on the tar pits. I write this for anyone who needs to hear it. I weep with a heart full of gratitude to myself for having the courage to fight, and I send that courage to anyone else who needs it. I am so thankful that I did not give up. Instead, I told myself, "Maybe, I can hold on, wait and do it tomorrow." For me, that tomorrow never came. I want so badly for others who are plagued with this curse to be healed of it. If you are suicidal, I am so sorry for your life's sorrow. Keep going, I know you can make it out of this pit. 🖤

If you feel you are currently in this phase, please call the Suicide and Crisis Line at 988 immediately.

How has Phase 5 manifested in my life?

_____

_____

_____

PERSONALIZED SAFETY PLAN

If you find yourself in any of these phases of suicidal ideation, it is important to intervene as soon as possible. Prioritizing a safety plan can offer you the necessary support in the face of a crisis, which is especially important when hopelessness and despair narrow your field of vision. The immediate moments around suicide are short, but the impact of suicide attempts gone wrong can lead to lasting harm both physically and emotionally. So many people who have attempted suicide and survived reported that they quickly regretted their decisions the moment their lives were in danger. At the core of suicidal ideation is not the desire to die but, rather, the desire not to suffer.

A personalized safety plan can be a resource at times when suffering makes you feel there are no options or hope. You might try thinking of people, places, and things that provide what you need when you are at your worst. Try to be as detailed as possible. If you are willing, share this safety plan with a trusted friend, therapist, or family member.

Remaining aware of the warning signs that you are experiencing an increase in suicidal thoughts or are feeling unsafe is a critical component to an effective safety plan. The following questions are designed to increase insight for when these moments occur. ☙

My Safety Plan

This Is Me, and I Am Here.

Name: _____

What are at least three warning signs that I am in crisis (thoughts, feelings, moods, situations, behavior)?

1. _____

2. _____

3. _____

What are at least three internal coping strategies (e.g., meditation, chanting, positive thinking, grounding skills like counting) I can do?

1. _____
2. _____
3. _____

What are at least three external coping strategies (e.g., dancing, running, taking a bath) I can do?

1. _____
2. _____
3. _____

What items should I keep out of my environment to ensure safety (e.g., alcohol, guns, prescription medications)?

1. _____
2. _____
3. _____

What can I add into my environment to increase a sense of safety (e.g., candles, photos of a loved one, inspirational quotes)?

1. _____
2. _____
3. _____

What are at least three social spaces I consider safe that I can go to?

1. _____
2. _____
3. _____

People I can ask for help:

Name _____

     Phone _____

Name _____

     Phone _____

Name _____

     Phone _____

In the case of a crisis, the professionals or agencies to contact are:

Therapist or clinician _____

     Phone _____

Guardian or emergency contact _____

     Phone _____

Local emergency service _____

     Phone _____

A good place to keep your safety plan is in a Safety Box, which serves as a tangible item that can bring you back to the present moment and get you through an episode. Whatever you include in this box should make you feel unique and loved. Here are some example items:

- Letters to yourself or from those you love
- Pictures of memories that make you feel happy or loved
- Music, albums, or art that evoke joy
- Art supplies, so you can get creative
- Aromatherapy or candles that smell good
- Books that are easy and light and evoke a positive emotion, even if they are ones that you enjoyed as a child

- Crystals, rocks, and seashells that you can hold and feel their calming energy
- Glow lights with bright colors
- A journal and colored pens
- A soft blanket and a sleep mask
- Spiritual or religious artifacts that speak to you

The most important part of creating a safety plan is putting it to use. Keeping a copy of it visible in your space or reviewing it often can help further your intention to follow through with it. Research shows[30] that the use of safety plans dramatically reduces incidents of suicide. It is a form of self-care that also increases resilience. Following your personalized safety plan allows you to be proactive about self-care, as well as proactive about seeking the support you need to manage stress, increase wellness, and manage suicidal thoughts.

We want to offer you an internalized self-care skill you can add to your safety plan. Gina has personally experienced its healing power in the face of her own suicidal thoughts, and we hope it brings you the same sense of peace. ☙

SET THE TONE FOR THE DAY

Most of the trauma that I experienced as a child occurred at night. My sleep was interrupted so often, I now wake up every morning with various levels of anxiety or in a fight or flight mode. I now know this is a physiological part of my life that I do not blame myself for or respond to negatively. Instead, as soon as I open my eyes, I assess where I am (I usually have tightness in my chest and buzzing nerves) and begin my daily routine. I've gotten so used to this practice that, usually within fifteen seconds or so, I can feel the calm coming back. In minutes, I feel safer and more grounded, and I can start my morning. I try to give myself at least five to ten minutes to achieve this

30. Monika Ferguson et al., "The Effectiveness of the Safety Planning Intervention for Adults Experiencing Suicide-related Distress: A Systematic Review," *Archives of Suicide Research* 26, no. 3 (2022): 1022–1045, https://www.tandfonline.com/doi/abs/10.1080/13811118.2021.1915217.

comfort. If I am still feeling agitated, I will use the following potent energy routine that has been specifically created to help anyone who would like to feel the protective energy of spirit in collaboration with self. ☙

The Liberated Healer's "Zipper Energy Meditation" Daily Morning and Night Routine

In this meditation you will be "zipping" yourself up into a bubble of light energy around your body and auric field in the morning and in the evening. You will "unzip" to let the stagnant energy out and call in new energy for the night.

You do not need any prior meditation experience. By simply engaging your body and mind through acting, reading, or speaking these instructions, the routine will be created. In other words, you cannot do this wrong or incompletely. Let go of any ideas of doing it perfectly, doing it for the right amount of time, or anything that might create a false sense of effort. The spirit knows what to do if you lose your place. It is your dutiful partner. We suggest the first few times you be in a quiet space so you can see, hear, or feel the subtle shifts. Again, if you cannot, that is perfectly fine. The healing work is still happening.

Once familiar with the process, you can do this anywhere at any time that you might feel a need for an energetic bump of protection and grounding. If you cannot do any of the movements for whatever reason, you will still benefit by imagining the process.

The central or first vessel in us is our soul. . . . Since the human soul is a higher, spiritual substance, it receives an inflow directly from God. —Emanuel Swedenborg, Soul-Body Interaction 8

ZIPPING IN (Morning)

1. Upon waking, we need to shake off the stagnant energy from the night. Begin by standing up and gently moving your neck and shoulders. Shake your arms and your hands, then your hips and legs at a pace that feels good for you. Root to the Earth below you and crunch your toes. If it feels good, bend at your hips and swing your body from side to side while reaching for the floor. Note: Most animals tend to do their own version of this practice upon waking. They will shake off the energy, often starting at their heads and then all the way down through their tails or feet. We have lost this instinct and practice in our modern world, but it is very important in terms of energy.

2. Coming back to your bed or a seat in the room, sit in a comfortable position. Do not cross your arms or legs if possible, so as not to stop the flow of energy through bent extremities.

3. With closed eyes (or a soft gaze in front of you), turn the sides of your mouth up slightly (which in dialectical behavioral therapy is called a "half smile"). If this action feels forced, you can simply imagine doing so, allowing the healing energy of smiling to wash over you.

4. Say out loud or in your head, "Hello," repeating the word as many times as feels good to you. This does three things:

   - Brings you into the here and the now into the present time
   - Connects your mind, body, and spirit
   - Alerts any guides or angels you have around you that you are ready to work

5. Stretch your arms over your head and take notice of where the edges of your fingertips are. This is the top edge of the auric field you are working. Keeping your arms straight, slowly circle the entire field of energy around you like a large bubble, ending with your hands down near your seat.

6. With your feet on the ground, imagine you are bringing in energy from the Earth up through the center of your feet into your calves, your knees, your thighs, your hips, and your torso. This will ground you while cleaning out any stuck energy.

7. Focus now just above your head and imagine a vibrant rainbow of colors that grows into the bubble you created with your arms. No muted colors here—rather, the energy of glorious red, orange, yellow, green, blue, and purple.

8. Notice any specific areas of your body or energy field that feel stuck, tense, or in need of your attention. Send this rainbow of energy to that location in your body or mind.

9. Now imagine the power of golden sunlight growing just over your head and on the back of your neck.

   • You can say to yourself or out loud: "I call back my own life-force energy and highest vibration of light."
   • Imagine the golden light falls over you like a shower of energy
   • Stay here in this flow of light as long as needed. Once you feel energized and ready, move to the final step

10. Reach your arms straight out again above your head and grasp onto a giant imaginary zipper. Imagine zipping up the bubble around you with your new glorious energy.

11. Move throughout the rest of your day with this newfound energetic protection.

ZIPPING OUT (Evening)

Even though you have been zipped up and protected all day, your energy can still get stagnant. Return to this practice just before lying down for sleep.

1. Connecting with your body, shake from head to toe—this time to release tension carried throughout the day.

2. Coming back to your bed, or a seat in the room, sit in a comfortable position (or lie down if you want to use this as a practice to induce sleep).

3. Reach your arms straight out again above your head, reaching with your fingers for a giant zipper. Pull it open—imagine unzipping the entire bubble around you and letting out all the energy of your day.

4. With closed eyes (or a soft gaze in front of you), turn the sides of your mouth up slightly in a half smile.

5. Say out loud or in your head, "Goodnight," which:

   - Brings you into the here and the now into the present time
   - Connects your mind, body, and spirit
   - Alerts any guides or angels you have around you that you are ready for rest

6. Stretch your arms straight up over your head and circle your energetic bubble. Bring in fresh energy from the Earth up through the center of your feet into your calves, your knees, your thighs, your hips, and your torso.

7. Bring back your rainbow of colors into the bubble you created with your arms.

8. Notice any specific areas of your body or energy field that feel stuck, tense, or in need of your attention. Send this rainbow of energy to that location in your body or mind.

9. Imagine the warm glow of the moon growing just over your head and on the back of your neck.

   - You can say to yourself or out loud, "I invite rest and peace."
   - Stay here in this glow of the moonlight as long as needed
   - Follow your breath and invite the comfort of rest and sleep

CONCLUSION

As you began Part 1, you could imagine you had entered a dense forest full of twists and turns, with new things to learn and patterns to recognize. The forest may have been dark and deep at times, and there were likely moments you feared you would never come out the other side. This was the forest of suicidal ideation. Everything you learned during your journey through the forest is still with you, but now you can see a new horizon, one of healing and new possibilities. In Part 2: The How of Healing, we will stand with you, unfold the map and help you find the trailheads guiding you toward your healing journey out of suicidal ideation.

PART 2

The How of Healing

Chapter 4: The Healing Journey

It is not our body that lives but our soul; our body receives life through our soul. Our actual life force, or actual vitality, comes from heavenly love. —Emanuel Swedenborg, Secrets of Heaven 1436

 WE NOW ENTER the next part of your journey—that of healing. Coming from the forest of suicidal ideation, we are now on its far edge and can see a horizon of healing. Though it might feel far away, the potential for healing is real and there are many pathways that can take you there. We will arrive first at the **5 Phases of Healing,** which include:

Phase 1: Realization

Phase 2: Clarity

Phase 3: Motivation

Phase 4: Resilience

Phase 5: Confidence

In the other chapters of Part 2, you will be offered an array of possible pathways to chart your course of healing. Evidence-based therapies, alternative therapies, and assorted techniques and meditations will be explored, and we encourage you to explore this section as you feel called, following your own heart and intuition. What you learn in Part 2 will serve as a resource to come back to as you make your way across the terrain of your healing journey.

Much like any change, nothing is completely linear in this journey, and you may find yourself wavering between phases. As life can become marred with suffering, there will likely be days when the depths of despair and suicidal thoughts are awakened, but when firmly planted in the phases of healing, you will have a vantage point of insight allowing you to recognize what is happening and to move back toward what or who brings you the greatest sense of peace. Essentially, you will more acutely feel the temporary nature of suicidal thoughts. You may even experience a phase of grieving suicidal thoughts as a coping skill. As we will explore in the section on parts (page 104), this may be a part of you that existed for a long time and that was trying to protect you, even if the methods were harmful.

Stepping outside yourself and receiving wisdom and support through forms of healing from others (whether with people or through spiritual entities that you are drawn to) is all a part of healing. We urge you not to allow it to be a solitary journey but rather, one of receiving. Each phase builds upon the other, and the next section explores each phase as experienced by Gina's story so that you can begin to reflect on how these phases have or will manifest in your own. ☙

The 5 Phases of Healing from Suicidality

PHASE 1: REALIZATION

The first step in healing from suicidal ideation is realizing and acknowledging the experience of these thoughts and feelings. This is a difficult step, but it is essential to be honest and take steps necessary to heal. More than likely, there is still a lot of confusion at this phase, while also recognizing one's personal ability to influence the future. Others may or may not be enlisted to help at this time. There is a desire to make a shift happen and let go—but the way is not entirely clear yet. Moving toward transformation can feel overwhelming, but recognizing patterns is important when on the healing journey. Many people will create their safety plans at this phase, if they have not done so already. It is common to feel both a little "stuck" and also excited at the same time. ☙

My Awareness Opens

My epiphany came after selling my home and gifting much of my money and belongings to others. Releasing the energetic hold that money held over me, my mind, body, spirit, and soul, gave me freedom. I understood that no matter what, I would be okay. I held all the power over what I allowed into my space. I had a choice to ingest fear or love. I understood I could believe what others said about me or ignore it.

I still had a lot of healing to do and periodically I fell back into old self-pity patterns and suicidal ideations, but they were less intense. I was "sick and tired of being sick and tired." I became my own cheerleader, visualizing myself strong enough to put my hand in a lion's mouth. I signed up for workshops and retreats on healing and spirituality. At those events, I met people who were dedicated to helping others. I realized there was a lot of love out there that I wasn't letting in. I experienced moments of profound happiness through these events and classes. While it didn't always happen, these carried me through and increased my desire to keep looking for more that resonated with me.

A friend invited me to a Hindu temple, and I tried Kundalini meditation for the first time. The class was all about energy. I felt outside of my body in the meditation but in a light and positive way. I felt like I was traveling in space where I could see stars, planets, and even black holes—but I never felt scared. In my mind, I flew over to Saturn, reached my hand out, and could touch the rings that went right through my fingertips. They were vibrant orange, yellow, and red, invigorating me with their energy. I was like a winged creature— superhuman—flying through the sky. I returned to my body, and I could only think, "Can I have more of that, please?" After this, my healing took a massive pivot in a liberating direction, and I wanted to know more about energy, spirit, and my capabilities. In this first phase of awareness, I was eager to learn as much as I could. That has never stopped.

PHASE 2: CLARITY

At this phase, clarity leads toward healthier choices, actions, and thinking. You are growing in your awareness that healing is not linear and is a multifaceted journey, so you continue to explore various ways to overcome suicidal ideation. This phase will still have ups and downs, but a foundation is forming; you are building the desire to continue living. When triggers are present, you have more awareness of them and a willingness to seek coping methods. You are increasing your ability to be vulnerable, and you may find that it feels easier to open up to others than it did in **Phase 1: Realization.** You experience a greater frequency of periodic moments of hope. You have more positive feelings as the numbing of the suicidal thoughts recedes. You might desire to engage in new or renewed forms of self-care such as dressing up a little, choosing a healthier diet, or reaching out to a friend you've ignored for a while. You don't feel the need to isolate as strongly; rather, you desire to be with others more than you did before.

Seeing The Path

My experience in this phase felt like I was fully committed to saving myself—becoming ingrained in who I was as a person. The shame

about needing or wanting help dissipated and I leaned into my excitement about the healing practices I was learning. My intuition sharpened and I could tell if a class or group resonated with me. Making these choices restored my power and sovereignty by building the ability to discern between what was right for me and what was not. I saw how special I was, that I was worthy of being here, and that I wanted to be here. I participated in a wide variety of yoga and meditation techniques. Occasional moments of suicidal ideation cropped up at this phase, but they were different. The episodes were brief and the harsh thoughts duller—they were losing power over me. Wounding from my traumas lingered, but I was in a better place to receive support.

During this phase, I still had a lot to work through. My mind was trained to play the victim. This is not to shame myself because I had real trauma, but I saw my life as a human JENGA tower, each block representing a person who did not see my value, put me down, or abused me. In the center of those blocks beat my precious, vulnerable heart. I was sometimes hard on myself running the storyline that "I should have known better." I questioned my life decisions. This is a lose/lose game. I realized: *I am a delicate human. I deserve compassion and empathy and if nobody will give it to me, I will have to gift it to myself.*

I let fewer people influence me in what I knew was not my truth. If I caught myself in old patterns, I remembered, "I have tools to help me through this." I returned to regular therapy and practiced daily centering meditations, walks in nature, salt baths, and yoga. I also researched audiobooks on the phases of grief, where I learned details about each phase and how they applied to what I was experiencing. Understanding these phases allowed me to intellectualize my pain instead of going straight to self-harm or negative self-talk. I felt a sense of pride, especially in how I was handling difficult situations. I looked to the heavens, angels, and guides and my source of light or God and sang songs of appreciation. People noticed a shift in me. My connections to others grew in their deepness and intensity. Some of these people had been there all along but I couldn't see them because I was blinded by my own self-hatred and pity. I could feel this all again; they were right there standing next to me, right where they have always been.

PHASE 3: MOTIVATION

At this phase, you feel less fear and despair. You are spending dedicated time engaging in chosen healing modalities, such as journaling or other activities, especially when triggers arise. You experience profound moments of understanding about why suicidal thoughts occurred; your insight motivates you to seek ways to heal these wounds. You find that you are living in the present more often than before, and you spend less time fixated on the past. This shift makes it easier to navigate obstacles as they arise. This phase commonly leads to moments of awakening as you uncover the root causes of your wounds. You have access to compassion and forgiveness toward yourself and others in a way that felt out of reach before. You feel motivated to make the necessary changes to your relationships, career, and old patterns. You take action to make these changes.

Driven to Heal

In my experience at this healing phase, an integration of the work shifted, affecting my daily decisions. Before this, I feared conflict because I worried it might result in another loss. I had long-standing

relationships with friends and acquaintances that were unhealthy. These became clear and I was able to walk away without fear or feeling I was the person in the wrong. I had one friend who would tell people I was a klutz and would repeat old stories of me falling into a hole or down the stairs. She would act like a clown when impersonating me and it always bothered me, but for years I let her do it. She seemed to relish when I would get in a bind, "Oh, there goes Gina again." When a new business venture failed, she said, "You have a fear of success." For years, I took her words at face value.

Now, not only do I stand taller physically but when I recognize behavior as toxic, I address it immediately. I speak about how it makes me feel, I listen without fierce judgment and we either get to a stronger plane of our relationship, or I let it go with love and grace. I made courageous moves to end situations that were not working for me. This cleansing process feels so good; it is the difference between eating an overprocessed fried meal or a delicious, fresh, organic piece of fruit.

In this third phase of healing, I started to own myself. My fear-based cycle of perpetual people-pleasing faded. *Lookout, world, here comes a new Gina! She is no longer interested in being on a hamster wheel of making sure everyone else is happy.*

When I gave myself this space, the right people, projects, and relationships appeared. They are entirely different, with boundaries rooted in respect. I imagine Emanuel Swedenborg saying to me,

"Hooray, you have found heavenly self-love! Give yourself a nice pat on the back.🐿

> *These two—spiritual warmth and spiritual light, or love and wisdom—flow together from God into the human soul, flow through our soul into our mind and its feelings and thoughts, and flow from there into our physical senses, speech, and actions.*
> —Emanuel Swedenborg, Soul-Body Interaction 8

PHASE 4: RESILIENCE

You experience more self-love in this phase, and in turn, you feel clearer on how to take care of yourself. You are able to recover from and withstand difficulties more easily. You more readily engage in self-care and seek support from others regularly. You have an increased feeling of connectedness to the world and form new relationships or reconnect with old ones. You feel a stronger sense of integration about the tools you use to support your ongoing healing (meditation, therapy, yoga). Your mind, body, spirit, and soul are working in sync more often, and the difference is palpable. Triggers carry less impact and almost never result in suicidal ideation. In addition to the healing work being done, you might be returning to hobbies, events, or practices that were once enjoyable. It is likely that you give more attention to protecting your resilience, which may mean you limit your exposure to content, people, situations, or conversations that do not support emotional growth, from a place of feeling centered in your wholeness.🐿

Feeling Different

At this phase, I explored clairvoyant and energy studies and how being highly sensitive affected me and my relationships. I learned that, by constantly worrying about what others thought, I was overtaxing my mental and physical body. Before this, I was fatigued, sickly, cloudy, and unable to make quality decisions. I identified

these imbalances and made changes with confidence; I spoke up for myself to ensure I was getting what I needed. I transitioned from student to teacher in important areas, giving me a sense of being "in service" to humanity. I was marching to my own tunes, and I loved them. This positive shift also drew more meaningful friendships, colleagues, and projects that resonated. I've had the joy of working on projects near and dear to my heart. This transformation from passive victim to advocate and guide has brought another level of healing altogether. ❧

PHASE 5: CONFIDENCE

At this phase, your positive self-talk becomes the norm, and you focus on self-care daily. You prioritize mental health with a sense of self-compassion. You have a deep understanding of how beautiful it is to be alive, despite life's hardships. You make self-empowered decisions more naturally, and you experience more hope, even in the case of a bad day. You feel an inner pull to search for deeper meaning and you focus on healing practices, treatments, or therapists in an expanded way. At this phase, you desire to help others overcome suffering. You experience gratitude more readily, and you feel genuine when smiling or interacting positively with others. You can identify your personal goals and what you want out of life with clarity. At times, you feel astonished by the amount of change that has occurred internally and externally. You have an ability to manifest your dreams and live fully in a way that once did not seem possible—a life free of pervasive suicidal ideation.

 Fierce and Free

Reflecting on this phase in my healing journey, it is challenging to pinpoint the exact moment I was aware I had arrived. Once, I was hiking and encountered a snake that had shed its skin. I thought how painful it must have been to push out of the old skin inch by inch, and how underneath the new skin is then so vulnerable to the elements. We often do not think much about this process, accepting that it is simply what a snake does. But in that moment on the trail, I felt that the snakeskin perfectly captured how I felt about my transformation. I had purposefully pulled each layer away to become a new version of myself. That shedding was incredibly painful; I had to strip away layers upon layers of suffering, habits, and storylines that did not align with my life. I chose my beautiful soul, embraced it, learned to care for it like the most valuable thing in the world. I struggled through healing, exploration, and discovery, and in the process, I shed layers of me that no longer contributed to the life I wanted and deserved. Much like the snake cannot return to its shed skin, I am forever changed and will never put on the old, lost layers. Through metamorphosis, I am shiny, brand new, and ready in this new transformational form. I came up with this saying a long time ago, but I never knew the true meaning until I arrived at this phase: "YOU are the JOY that nothing else is. Your SOUL is the most valuable thing you OWN. Take care of it."

As humans, we may face immense abuse, hardship, and fears but if we can meet the adversity with compassion, we will have known true divinity and our higher path. This enables us to realize our angelic soul-self, setting up a place where God can enter our heart and home. ☙

Reflection on the 5 Phases of Healing

In reflecting on these five phases, what parts appeal most to you?

_____

_____

_____

With which phase do you most resonate currently in your journey?

_____

_____

_____

If you feel stuck in the 5 Phases of Suicidal Ideation, what ideas can you take from these phases to lead you toward your path of healing?

_____

_____

_____

Hidden deep within the desires of every angel's heart there is a kind of current that draws her or his mind to do something. In that activity the mind finds its peace and satisfaction. This peace and satisfaction then condition the mind to be receptive to the love of being useful that flows in from the Lord. —Emanuel Swedenborg, True Christianity 735[6]

"I am Light" Meditation

(5–10 minutes)

After reflecting on the **5 Phases of Healing,** it can help to take some time in quiet meditation and reflection. The following practice engages you in the emotional and cognitive shifts that commonly occur in these healing phases, supporting your ability to experience a sense of inner light and love.

1. Sit comfortably, preferably cross-legged, with a cushion or blanket under your sit bones, with your back straight and your head slightly bent forward. Pull your shoulder blades together in the back. This helps to open the center of the chest. Rest your hands on your thighs with the palms facing upward and point your thumbs away from your body. Breathe naturally.

2. Close your eyes. Connect one hand to your heart and one to the belly. Say, out loud or in your mind, "I am light even though . . ." and add the things that are heavy on your heart. "I am loved even though . . ." and say another frustration or something you want to clear. You can repeat this a few times.

3. Imagine a bright ball over your head growing like a golden sun providing you warmth and light.

4. Imagine emotions or judgments you want to let go of being cast into the sun's light—burning away. Repeat this a few times until your energy feels like it has transformed, and you feel relaxed.

5. Hold your knees with your palms and gently rock on your sit bones as any negative energy leaves the base of your spine. If you want to

"hum" or sing "om" now, it will help to loosen more stuck energy in the body. After you have done this for a few minutes, stop.

6. Return to a comfortable seat and find stillness in your mind. Say thank you to yourself and extend gratitude for that moment.

7. Extend your legs and reach toward your toes. Shake your legs, roll your neck, and move in any way that feels good. Continue into your day or night with increased ease.

Chapter 5: Trailheads for Healing

Love is the essence that not only forms all things but also bonds and unites them to each other; therefore love is the force that holds all things in connection. —Emanuel Swedenborg, True Christianity *37*

gc WILL I EVER LOVE AGAIN?

In the early days after my husband left, I struggled to accept that my marriage was over. I was still looking over at the walnut tree that served as a memory of a marriage proposal and my thoughts of suicide. There was both shock and physical withdrawal, irrationally waiting for him to walk through the door and jump in bed with hugs and kisses. He was gone, his love and attention given to another. I wondered if my eyes would run out of tears, endlessly thankful for my dogs lying in bed with me for comfort.

What I've come to realize is when you love someone, that love never goes away. The relationship may be different, but the love is still there, and that is okay. I had to rework my thinking, which earlier was, "I was unworthy of love." That is not the case, we all want, need, and deserve love.

I would not have grown spiritually and wouldn't have found my life purpose had we stayed together. The hardship taught me how to stand on my own two feet. It forced me to find what could heal my wounds, traumas, and suicidal ideation. It was for me to fix, not anyone else. When I think about him now, I play one of his old songs, and dance wildly. I keep the loving memories and throw out the rest. Knowing that I was a part of such creativity is all my soul needed.

My Trailhead

During the loss of my marriage, I was moving through all the phases of suicidal ideation. Aside from a few close friends, I kept it all secret, held it in, not asking for help where I could have. Thankfully, I had my therapist, Dr. Stirling, who had a nondescript office in one of the most smoldering hot parts of Southern California, and I loved this space because it was always dark and cool. He collected geodes and fossils, and I enjoyed looking at them when I felt triggered. My artwork had similar patterns as his fossils, calming my mind. He encouraged me to use art in session, sometimes almost breaking the pen with the intensity of my emotion. He helped me understand my art was an expression of my feelings and energies on paper. I would turn to it whenever I couldn't express how I felt in words. My art has evolved as I healed but I always feel the calmest and most connected when drawing.

Dr. Stirling was kind and never made me feel insecure about oversharing. He even encouraged it. For the first time in my life, I felt like my voice mattered. He asked, "Gina, when did you, this wondrous human spirit and soul, begin to think, 'I should just die'?"

In his profound wisdom, he explained how these negative thoughts were not originally my own but were instead a result of my mind and body being traumatized. He assured me that what I experienced was not a safe or normal childhood. I learned that when I was a child, I should have been told things such as, "You are worthy, we love you, we will keep you safe, and listen when you need to express your feelings." Dr. Stirling exposed the extent to which my past influenced me and how it was causing my negative self-talk. I cried when he said, "We will begin your therapy with the absolute clarity that this trauma is not yours to carry. This programming is the crux of a distorted belief system that led you to chronic suicidal ideation."

As we worked through my pain, I would sometimes cry out in sessions, "What's wrong with me? Am I crazy?" He assured me that I was not, and that I was a trauma survivor. We would practice rewording my spoken words into, "I have experienced trauma, and the work I am doing is valuable and difficult, and it is leading me toward healing."

The practice of reframing my self-talk made me understand they were a result of my trauma. For the first time I truly started to believe I could change and heal, allowing me to live a more balanced and happy life. ♡

CHOOSING YOUR TRAILHEAD

Much like a trailhead marks the beginning of a path, this next section serves as the starting point for learning the **5 Phases of Healing from Suicidality.** From there, we will guide you in learning useful techniques to add to your toolbox for navigating your path toward healing. The skills explored will cover three evidence-based therapies: dialectical behavioral therapy, acceptance and commitment therapy, and the Internal Family Systems model; as well as several alternative therapies that Gina found particularly helpful in her healing journey. Not only will you learn how and why these therapies can provide direction on your healing journey, but you will have the opportunity to try specific skills based on these approaches. You will be able to address your personal experience with suicidal ideation and promote forward movement on your path toward recovery. These trailheads for healing are a handful of many possibilities. We invite you to find your way by seeing which therapies or techniques spark your interest or curiosity.

THREE EVIDENCE-BASED THERAPIES
Dialectical Behavioral Therapy

Once you find a therapist who feels like the right fit, and for some this can take many tries, the therapist will likely suggest several therapy approaches to address suicide. One of the most effective evidenced-based therapies for preventing suicide is dialectical behavioral therapy (DBT) developed in the 1970s by American psychologist Marsha Linehan.[31] DBT was initially developed to help treat those with personality disorders, manage intense emotions, and improve interpersonal relationships. According to the Mayo Clinic,[32] DBT has been proven effective to treat:

- Self-harm
- Suicidal behaviors
- PTSD
- Substance-use disorders
- Eating disorders, most specifically binge eating and bulimia
- Depression
- Anxiety

One of the reasons why DBT is so effective for treating suicide is that one of its goals is to help keep clients out of the hospital. There is little research supporting hospitalization for preventing suicide, and in fact, the stress of hospitalization can cause further risk factors. Consistent monitoring of suicide risk with the use of diary cards is an important part of DBT therapy and allows the therapist to support healthy management of unwanted emotions, thoughts, sensations, or self-harm. Objective self-reflection is one of the most helpful aspects of the diary cards. It allows you to identify whether you are engaging in recovery skills as opposed to risk-inducing behaviors, without being judgmental of your experience.

31. Marsha Linehan, *DBT Skills Training Manual* (New York: Guilford Publications, 2014).
32. Mayo Clinic Staff, "Tests and Procedures: Psychotherapy," *Mayo Clinic*. April 11, 2023, https://www.mayoclinic.org/tests-procedures/psychotherapy/about/pac-20384616.

Skills in Action DBT Diary Card

Below you will find a simplified version of the DBT diary card. Each DBT skill has been described by how it would present in action. Take a moment to reflect on the previous day and circle any healthy coping DBT skills you employed at least once during that day. Continue using the card to help increase insight about the rest of your week.

DBT Skills in Action							
1. Wise mind (having both reason and emotion in your thinking)	Mon	Tues	Wed	Thurs	Fri	Sat	Sun
2. Observe: notice unhealthy urges rise and fall (riding the urge wave)	Mon	Tues	Wed	Thurs	Fri	Sat	Sun
3. Describe: experiences and feelings (to yourself or others)	Mon	Tues	Wed	Thurs	Fri	Sat	Sun
4. Participate in opportunities (social or otherwise)	Mon	Tues	Wed	Thurs	Fri	Sat	Sun
5. Remain nonjudgmental of the self (thinking about and speaking to yourself kindly)	Mon	Tues	Wed	Thurs	Fri	Sat	Sun
6. Remain mindful and in the moment	Mon	Tues	Wed	Thurs	Fri	Sat	Sun
7. Build positive experiences by saying yes to opportunities	Mon	Tues	Wed	Thurs	Fri	Sat	Sun
8. Self-soothe with skills of your choice (such as prayer, meditation, exercise, journaling, breath skills)	Mon	Tues	Wed	Thurs	Fri	Sat	Sun

DBT Skills in Action							
9. Weigh pros and cons in decision making	Mon	Tues	Wed	Thurs	Fri	Sat	Sun
10. Practice radical acceptance: notice pain without resisting it	Mon	Tues	Wed	Thurs	Fri	Sat	Sun
11. Building structure in your work	Mon	Tues	Wed	Thurs	Fri	Sat	Sun
12. Building structure in your relationships	Mon	Tues	Wed	Thurs	Fri	Sat	Sun
13. Building structure with your time	Mon	Tues	Wed	Thurs	Fri	Sat	Sun
14. Building structure in your physical space	Mon	Tues	Wed	Thurs	Fri	Sat	Sun
15. Use a self-compassionate tone when thinking or speaking	Mon	Tues	Wed	Thurs	Fri	Sat	Sun
16. Recognize failings as room to grown (growth mindset)	Mon	Tues	Wed	Thurs	Fri	Sat	Sun
17. Express your needs	Mon	Tues	Wed	Thurs	Fri	Sat	Sun
18. Set a boundary (with yourself or others)	Mon	Tues	Wed	Thurs	Fri	Sat	Sun

Next, identify any difficult emotions, suicidal thoughts, or self-harm behaviors you engaged in this past week. Using the score key below, identify whether you employed any of the previously mentioned DBT skills to support yourself. You can use this card for personal reflection or share it with a support person or mental health provider.

Date	Urges to . . .		Emotions								
	Suicide	Self-Harm	Pain	Sad	Shame	Anger	Fear	Disgust	Envy	Jealous	Guilt
	0–5	0–5	0–5	0–5	0–5	0–5	0–5	0–5	0–5	0–5	0–5
Mon											
Tues											
Wed											
Thur											
Fri											
Sat											
Sun											

Date	Actions			
	Self-Harm	Lying	Joy	Skills
	Y/N	#	0–5	0–7
Mon				
Tues				
Wed				
Thur				
Fri				
Sat				
Sun				

Score Key

Used Skills

0 = Not thought about or used

1 = Thought about, not used, didn't want to

2 = Thought about, not used, wanted to

3 = Tried but couldn't use them

4 = Tried, could do them, but they didn't help

5 = Tried, could use them, helped

6 = Didn't try, used them, didn't help

7 = Didn't try, used them, helped

Keeping a diary helps you gain control of suicidal thoughts and improve your mood by helping you prioritize issues and concerns. Tracking symptoms day to day can help you recognize triggers, as well as provide awareness of what skills help you better control them.

Notes

_____

_____

_____

_____

_____

Radical Acceptance (ACT) and Suicide

As you become more aware of your emotions and urges around suicide, you will likely encounter distressing memories, sensations, thoughts, and feelings. As a society, our typical response to pain has been to try to fix or avoid it, but what if we stopped running and faced it head-on?

These were the questions asked to psychologist Steven D. Hayes in the 1980s.[33] He created acceptance and commitment therapy (ACT) to heal from his experience with panic attacks. This action-oriented therapy approach stems from both cognitive and behavioral therapies. At its core, ACT encourages us not to ignore or deny the presence of suicidal thoughts, along with the pain that causes them, but rather, teaches us how to mindfully accept our full range of emotions as they are.

As the renowned Swiss psychiatrist Carl Jung stated in his book *Wounded Healer of the Soul*,[34] "What we resist persists," and the same is true of suicidal thoughts. I see this often with my therapy clients,

33. Russ Harris, ACT *Made Simple: An Easy-to-read Primer on Acceptance and Commitment Therapy* (New Harbinger Publications, 2019).
34. Claire Dunne, *Carl Jung: Wounded Healer of the Soul* (Watkins Media Limited, 2015).

where the anticipatory anxiety surrounding suffering can become more painful than the actual issue. My clients who have chosen to embody acceptance imagine they are placing their suffering or distress into a metaphoric backpack. They accept they cannot take this backpack off and acknowledge its existence but then choose to continue living despite it.

For some, it can be difficult to imagine living life amidst painful thoughts or sensations, and so, using the four ACT mindfulness skills can be very helpful:

- Acceptance: of the presences of inner experiences, urges, memories, or sensations

- Cognitive defusion: noticing thoughts as separate entities that can come and go as opposed to over attaching or personifying them (i.e., I am experiencing anxiety, not, I am anxious)

- Contact with the present moment: attunement to what is happening in the here and now (i.e., I feel immense pain over my trauma, but at this exact moment I am sitting in my home trying to read a book; the book is about . . .)

- Observing self: notice the noticing! You are the person experiencing your feelings and inner world; this helps to dissolve the hold pain can have over us

Experiencing suicidal thoughts can often lead to self-defeating stories about oneself. This causes us to feel blended with our pain and suffering, making it difficult to stay in the present moment. When these stories arise, you can choose to employ ACT therapy's four mindfulness skills with the following exercise.✂

Thank Your Mind and Name Your Stories

For this exercise, ensure that you remain nonjudgmental and self-compassionate in your tone, whether speaking out loud or in your mind. One suggestion is to slow down the rate and volume you speak, allowing for a more soothing vocal tone. This opposes our natural tendency to accelerate in pitch and speed when under stress. When in distress or experiencing suicidal thoughts, try the following:

1. Acknowledge the thought's presence, allowing it to exist (acceptance).

2. Recognize the thought as a product of your mind and thank your mind for its opinion (cognitive defusion).

3. Take notice of exactly where you are while creating this story (contact with the present moment).

4. For each negative narrative you hold about yourself in that moment (or in relation to a situation), name that narrative as you would the title of a story, such as:

   • This is my anxiety story.
   • This is the story about not feeling accepted.
   • This is the story where I contemplate suicide.

5. Finally, thank your mind for recognizing the story (observing self), and allow the story to play in the distant background while you re-engage with whatever task or situation you have in front of you—even if that situation is trying to get to sleep—as these stories tend to play loudly in quiet moments.

6. If the story returns, thank your mind for noticing and connect back with the present moment or task at hand.

 ### Accept and Love Everything

For me, radical acceptance has been challenging to learn and fully realize, as all difficult lessons can be. Yet, it's absolutely been the most rewarding therapy I have embodied. I found that without radical acceptance, I remained in the past. If you are living in the past, how can you also be fully living in the present?

Sometimes I am determined and stubborn, certain I can change or manipulate a situation to avoid the inevitable pain. For example, I might shower someone with love and affection when I fear they are pulling away, instead of accepting what is happening. I too might even want to pull away from them, but the fear of being rejected or suffering another failed relationship keeps me striving instead of seeing the reality of what is happening. The result is often similar; I lose months and even years staying in spaces that I knew were wrong for me, all because of fear.

Now, practicing radical acceptance and commitment therapy, I more often analyze my situations and see them for what they are and not for what I want them to be. Intuitively, I know the right choice for me. While I still sometimes struggle to accept that something or someone is not good for me, I know that if I choose radical acceptance I can understand myself, my past traumas, and situations much better. This leaves me feeling more confident, knowing that tomorrow is a new day. I can choose to accept and love myself without judgment and remain fully committed to this reality. ♥

> *The life in our will is the goodness of love, and its offshoots are called feelings. The life in our understanding is the truth that leads to wisdom, and its offshoots are called thoughts. Our mind is alive as a result of our feelings and thoughts. —Emanuel Swedenborg,* Soul-Body Interaction 8

 Safety for All Parts of You: Internal Family Systems

For some, the idea of being made up of multiple parts can be difficult to understand. Descartes famously said, "I think therefore I am," which describes how we form our sense of reality and existence through our thoughts and self-referential perception. But what if it is not just one unified "I" but instead, a collective "we"? This would mean that when we think, feel, or do something that seems out of character, it is a result of a part of us, not the whole of us. This allows us to take a step back and examine our behaviors and experiences from a growth mindset, as opposed to over-identifying with every unhealthy thought or reaction we have.

Richard Schwartz, founder of the Internal Family Systems model (IFS),[35] proposes that we are made up of a collection of subpersonalities interacting to create our intrapsychic realm. Schwartz conceptualizes that each of us consists of an inner family of parts that fulfill different roles, both healthy and unhealthy, making up our holistic "system." While there is no limit to how many unique parts we can have, at the center we all possess a "Self" that is most present when we are connected to our authentic core. Thomas Holmes, author of *Parts Work: An Illustrated Guide to Your Inner Life*,[36] describes the Self as the living room where all other parts gather to be in relationship with each other. Self can be a loving, wise guide in that room or just the feeling of the warm, safe space itself. Ideally, when we are leading with the Self, we are expressing our authentic needs without being threatened or overwhelmed (flooded) by other parts within our system.

Fundamental to this theory is that threats from a part that is making unhealthy choices does not mean this part is inherently bad or needs to be extricated from the system; rather, this unhealthy part needs to be paid attention to and more effectively understood. Within IFS, suicidality is not just an experience; it signals a part and the

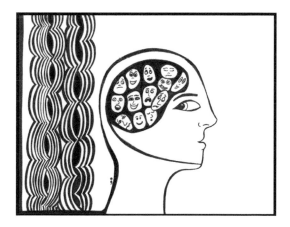

35. Richard C. Schwartz and Martha Sweezy, *Internal Family Systems Therapy,* Second edition (New York: The Guilford Press, 2020).
36. Thomas Holmes et al., *Parts Work: An Illustrated Guide to Your Inner Life* (Kalamazoo: Winged Heart Press, 2007).

suicidality is the protective role that part has taken on. The roles our parts play fall into three categories: managers, firefighters, and exiles. Understanding not only which part you are interacting with but also what protective role it plays allows you to engage in the forms of self-therapy that will be explored in this chapter.

Mapping the Inner System of Parts

MANAGERS

The purpose of managers is to help dictate how the person interacts with their external world to keep them from being hurt by others. This part's goal is to prevent pain or trauma through behaviors that can sometimes embody a sense of control or at times mastery. Examples of manager roles can be the caretaker, the critical part, the people-pleaser, the perfectionist, and other forms of self-protection. Personifications of these roles may look like neat freaks, over-controlling parents, workaholics, or overachievers.

FIREFIGHTERS

The purpose of firefighters is to prevent pain and unwanted experiences, as well as sensations and emotions, through reactive behaviors. Examples include being impulsive, risk-taking, or dissociating. Firefighters are highly focused on the present and struggle to imagine experiences beyond the here and now, especially when it comes to distress or pain. Personification of these roles may look like substance abuse, emotional or disordered eating, compulsive spending, isolation, self-harm such as cutting, or extreme defensiveness. The suicidal part is most connected to the firefighter role. It acts as an internal hero who surfaces at the most desperate times, in an effort to seek relief from the emotional pain and despair experienced by the system.

EXILES

Our exiles are the parts that the firefighters and managers are trying to protect the system from. They encompass our past trauma, shame, self-loathing, pain, and negative self-talk. They are often kept in the background and are at times unknown, as the protective parts have worked hard to keep them at bay. To truly integrate into a well-balanced person (system), exiles need to be acknowledged. When they are ignored, these parts will break through the surface at times when our other protective parts are fatigued or overwhelmed from their efforts. Exiles want to be heard and healed, and often, the most helpful part to help facilitate this is the Self.

Being able to identify which part of you is reacting helps empower your ability to learn from, work with, and care for your part. For example, if you are overmanaging an exile related to insecurity with the perfectionist manager, this will likely result in a firefighter (such as the suicidal part) surfacing to try and extinguish pain as quickly as possible. By connecting with your insecurity and supporting that part of you, the manager does not have to work so hard, meaning the firefighter (suicidal part) does not either. 🐿

Exploring Your Parts

The IFS wheel pictured here can support you in exploring your own parts. As mentioned, there is no limit to how many parts can exist within each protective role. With compassionate curiosity, use this drawing or a separate page to write down any parts that you are currently aware of in their respective spaces in the wheel. In the space marked as "Self," you can identify thoughts or sensations you experience when you feel most centered, which we will explore next in this chapter.

As you continue to pay attention to your parts, you will likely discover more. You can add more to your wheel in the future, create a new one, or simply take notice of the part and its role in your life.

> *Something that appears like a soul and a body exists in every facet of our being—in every facet of our feelings and in every facet of our thinking.—Emanuel Swedenborg,* Secrets of Heaven *1910*

I HAVE PARTS?

In writing about my different parts, I can't help but think of the book *Sybil,* written by Flora Rheta Schreiber in 1973.[37] I clearly remember reading this book in my youth and watching Sally Field's performance in the 1976 film as a six-year-old. The film made a big impact on my life. I recall being scared by this character and people like her. I wondered if I had any of these parts. When I first learned of IFS and parts work, I began to understand how identifying and personifying my parts would give me the ability not to have to take on the whole of my issues but to gently work on the bits a little at a time. It helped me create a more robust version of myself. It felt good to know that the parts of me I thought of as bad or broken had a role in trying to protect me. Through exploration I came to realize that these parts were not the enemy.

Through engaging in parts work, I have uncovered two exiled parts that were most connected to my suicidal ideation. The first is a bully part who would degrade me over any mistake or egregious error. This part cared more about how everyone else was experiencing me, even at my own expense. I felt cemented to this part, and I could not escape it. My internal loop was, "I'm uneducated, stupid, untalented, and useless." I was a very deep feeler, but I had to hide that part of myself, especially in my professional life, as I wanted to be taken seriously.

The second part was the unworthy part, who would sabotage good relationships, constantly taunting me into the tar pit of self-pity. Its internal loop said to me, "You're ugly, unlovable, undeserving, unwanted, and worthless." This part of me feared Sundays because those were my loneliest days, especially when my husband would be on tour

---

37. Flora Rheta Schreiber, *Sybil: The Classic True Story of a Woman Possessed by Sixteen Separate Personalities* (Regnery Publishing, 1973).

for several months. Before I dove in and worked on myself, Sundays were terrifying.

The term "frenemy" (a person who is ostensibly friendly or collegial but who is antagonistic, competitive, and your enemy) is a great way to explain how these parts made me feel. My frenemy was not someone I could walk away from because it was within myself. At the time, I wished I could kill off these two parts, and so, the suicidal part became the heroic firefighter rushing in to protect me from these exiles. It led me to believe that ending my life would end the suffering I was experiencing.

Then there were my managers, the overachiever and a workaholic who I noticed would cautiously micromanage my life in an effort to make me appear more high functioning than I felt. These managers ensured that I never went on vacations or took time off because I would have missed essential work opportunities. While these managers brought superficial success, I came to understand that they were not leaving me any room for joy. Giving these parts room to breathe and let go liberated me, allowing me to enjoy my life in the way that best served me. Another manager that I still struggle with is the overgiver, who I must often check in with. This part is the first to volunteer anytime someone needs something, even if it is not in my best interest. Now I have learned that constantly giving my energy, money, and positive attention can take away a true connection with all parts of me. I need support, too, and that means not depleting myself. At this point in my life, I try to connect with my whole system every day, even the suicidal part, which helps me achieve a sense of balance, understanding, and self-love, even when things are tough. ♡

 ### Balancing all the Parts
There are several IFS techniques that can help you overcome suicidal ideation, experience joy, and learn what it is you truly need to heal. Some ideas include guided meditations where you meet with and speak to your parts, journaling where you speak on behalf of different parts or even write letters to each separate one, or art where

you create images of each part to better understand them. All of these approaches help create harmony for your various parts. When your parts are working harmoniously together, IFS calls this being integrated, meaning that one's Self is in the driver's seat, and other parts are being attended to when needed. You make choices that feel authentic, you speak to yourself with self-compassion, and you are able to deal with adversity and stress without feeling triggered.

When a part, such as the suicidal part, is overfunctioning and flooding the system, it is often trying to protect you from an exile full of painful feelings you've buried. It becomes difficult to hear the Self, and the suicidal part may convince you that you truly want to die. Allowing a protector to make a permanent choice like this without learning all the reasons why they feel the way they do does not honor you as a whole person, nor does it give the protector what it actually wants and needs: a sense of safety and peace.

How we speak to ourselves has a dramatic impact on our internal experience, as well as on how we see ourselves in the world and within our relationships. In *Fierce Self-Compassion: How Women Can Harness Kindness to Speak Up, Claim Their Power, and Thrive,*[38] Dr. Kristin Neff, author and educator on the topic, describes self-compassion as holding ourselves with kindness and understanding when we suffer, instead of beating ourselves up inwardly or ignoring the pain. At the heart of self-compassion is the ability to remain curious about our parts, as opposed to critical; otherwise, we risk not knowing them and what they need. What we say to our parts and how we approach them plays a role in whether they will remain present and heal. Much like someone who we value as a close friend, being mindful of how you approach them defines our level of intimacy and understanding of one another. To connect more readily with yourself and learn about your suicidal part, the following are compassionate reframes to encourage exploration.♥

38. Kristin Neff, *Fierce Self-Compassion: How Women Can Harness Kindness to Speak Up, Claim Their Power, and Thrive* (London: Penguin Books Limited, 2021).

SELF-COMPASSION AND CURIOSITY FOR OUR PARTS

Take a moment to reflect on each question and try answering from either the suicidal part or another part that is suffering and wants to be heard.

1. What are you afraid will happen if you live?

2. When do you feel the least suicidal?

3. What needs do you have that are not being met?

4. How would it feel to let go of the burden of having to fix all the suffering?

5. What do you need to feel you can relax a bit more and let go of some of your responsibilities?

Your Self

MY PARTS ARE THE REAL ROCKSTARS

I appreciate how IFS promotes this idea of a balanced and whole system and diminishes the negative thinking of being broken or separate from the self. Reaching the point where I understood that I was one holistic system and that all my parts have value was the beginning of my transformational healing. When I was suicidal, my Self felt wholly separated, like I was hovering outside my energy field. This disconnection is scary and can be omnipresent during **Phase 4: Intent,** and **Phase 5: Action** of suicidal ideation.

Divorce is never easy. During mine, my entire outward identity about being married to the love of my life shattered all around me. I was incredibly suicidal during this time, but I thought I could fix it by using one of my managers. My overworked manager would ensure that I worked overtime and kept myself from feeling and healing the things I needed to really be working on. My denial was at level ten. That is why when one of the cofounders at the agency I worked for seemed to fancy me, I entertained the thought. It was Christmas and my first holiday away from my husband. I went to a party and the cofounder was there. I admit that I am not good with large amounts of alcohol (much to the chagrin of my Irish family). I drank too much at the party, which I realize now was likely a firefighter risk-taker part of me that was trying to help me cope with my complex feelings.

Despite knowing I was too drunk, the cofounder took me home, which was the last thing I remember until I woke up the following day—still feeling inebriated and, then, also violated. This situation set off a domino reaction that changed the course of my life. My career meant everything to me, and now, I feared it was in danger. I wasn't in denial any longer; I needed help if I were to survive, and Dr. Stirling was a big key during this timeframe specifically. Despite preconceived notions I had around therapy from earlier in my life, I knew that this was what I needed and could potentially change my life. I dedicated myself to the experience with vigor and wished it had not taken me thirty-three years to take care of myself in that way.

Dr. Stirling and I worked on pulling back the veil I had created around myself. He helped me to understand how all these situations and parts worked together to make me what I had become. He encouraged me to gently address each part and understand why they were created. Many of these parts came from when I was a child to help me survive. He helped me understand how now they needed to evolve to work with the person I was at that moment. I was able to safely explore my physical reactions, which were triggered by shame, regret, and judgment. I was able to explore why my throat contracted, my hands shook, and my head burned whenever I tried to speak about suicidal thoughts, triggers, or abuse. Through working with my parts, I was able to understand my reaction and even honor and express gratitude for what they were trying to do for me. As a result, even the suicidal parts began to dissipate, and my Self-energy was able to take charge much more often. I was now able to transmute the things that were no longer serving me and lean into what was. These special people who help others learn to work with and love their parts, like Dr. Amelia Kelley, are my heroes.

Two specific Internal Family Systems tools that were shared with me in therapy that I found transformative were the "8 Cs" and the "5 Ps," which you can find below. 🍃

THE QUALITIES OF SELF
THE "8 Cs"

Compassion: I must have compassion for all parts of me and give them what they need.

Curiosity: It is my mind, body, and soul that is going to benefit from understanding deeply the process of integrating my parts. Be curious and learn.

Courage: I am familiar with the experience of hitting a wall and having no idea how I will get over it. This is when I must call upon a courage deep inside of me to help get me over the wall and to the other side.

Clarity: It is nearly impossible to work with parts of myself without understanding them. To achieve clarity and space, I must keep my body and mind clear by nourishing them with healthy foods, hydration, and proper rest. I should also try to surround myself with positive people.

Creativity: I can choose to be limitless by remaining open to thinking outside the box and being receptive to my imagination.

Connected: I might not agree with or understand everything my parts have to offer at first, but if I listen to the best of my ability and digest what I can, I will connect deeply to the material and those offering it.

Confidence: I know that I belong here. I am special. I am unique and like no one else. I deserve all the same love and accolades I would give to another being, animal, or ideology.

Calm: I will stay grounded. Peace is a process, but it will come.

THE "5 Ps"

Presence: I remain in the present moment as much as possible, rather than fixating on the past or future, where I cannot change or predict outcomes.

Persistence: Nothing done well is achieved without practicing and repeating it daily.

Perspective: Perspective alters my experience, and I have the ability to change this through shifting my narrative any time. Being human can be challenging, but I have more power than I know.

Playfulness: Laughter and play are energies of the highest vibration. Whenever I need to break through a dark spot and into the light, I will choose to go play immediately. (Adults do not play enough and need it just as much as children.) I will try to remember something I loved to do as a child, such as drawing, dancing, or watching cartoons. Anything that makes me feel light and alive will work.

Patience: All great accomplishments take time. To know patience is to deeply know myself.

A few words are needed to show how matters stand here, specifically how they stand with human beings. A human being is nothing else but an organ or vessel that receives life from the Lord; we do not live on our own. . . . The life that flows into us from the Lord comes from his divine love. This love, or the life that radiates from it, flows in and bestows itself on the vessels in

> *our rational and earthly minds. Such vessels in us face away from the life force because of the evil we inherit by birth and the evil we ourselves acquire by committing it. However, so far as it can do so, the inflowing life repositions the vessels to receive itself.*
> —Emanuel Swedenborg, Secrets of Heaven 3318:2

IFS Meditation—Working with Your Suicidal Part

Meditation and mindfulness are the most important practices for connecting with your parts. Taking the time to go inward provides connection with the Self-energy that allows you to work with and heal your suicidal part. You can set aside time to do IFS meditation regularly as preventive care, or you can use the following meditation inspired by Schwartz's work. Use these practices at any point when the suicidal part overwhelms your thoughts, behaviors, or emotions. If you are feeling deeply dysregulated, return to the EMDR Spiral Skill from Chapter 2 first (page 56), before doing this exercise.

- Begin by connecting with your body and noticing any physical sensations you are experiencing related to your suicidal part. Rate the distress (SUDS) from 1 to 10.

- If you feel comfortable, close your eyes and take a moment to connect with your body.

- Try to find a quiet space within yourself that feels grounded, neutral, and soft. Many find pressing their feet into the ground helpful, if necessary.

- Become aware of your breath. If it feels good, take a slow deep breath in, filling your lungs to the base of your belly. On the exhale, allow any tension from your shoulders, neck, and back body to relax. Then return to natural breathing.

- Next, imagine a room with a long wall of windows that you are standing outside of, looking in from a safe, peaceful distance. Notice everything within the room.

- Next, invite your suicidal part to walk into the room. Notice any sensations or reactions. Remain curious.

- Notice everything you can about this part, including its age, how it looks, its size, and its energy.

- Ask yourself how you feel about this part. Try to remain curious (at least somewhat), so this part feels safe communicating. If you notice intense negative reactions (or parts) that surface, invite these parts to step away for the rest of the meditation.

- If you would like, you can enter the room with the suicidal part or, if preferred, remain outside looking through the windows.

- Look at them, if possible, in their eyes. Let them know you are not trying to get rid of them but, rather, just trying to learn more about them.

- When you are ready, ask them the following questions, taking time to allow for each reply. You can even ask them to "Tell me more" if you feel they are holding back.

  - Can you tell me your story?
  - When did you first come to be?
  - What do you feel your job is for me?
  - What are you afraid will happen if you don't do your job? (This is the burden they carry.)

Write down any of the responses you would like to note here.

_____

_____

_____

- Finally, close this experience by expressing gratitude to them for the work they've done. Remind them that they can continue to let go of the burdens they carry and that you will check in with them with moments of mindfulness when they need you.

- If you want to spend more time with this part, do so. You can imagine playing with them (especially if they are a child part), embracing them, or just being with one another.

- Now connect back with your breath and place your hands on your heart center. Thank yourself for being so brave and willing to learn more about your suicidal part and their journey.

This powerful meditation can be used with all of your parts. If you do not have the time and space available to do the entire meditation, you can choose a brief version with these simple steps.

1. Notice what you feel in your body and rate it from 1 to 10.

2. Notice which part is asking for attention.

3. Ask what it is it wants and needs at that moment and listen with curiosity.

4. Use at least three inhales and exhales to help unburden this part, and invite the Self-energy to become more present.

5. Thank this part for showing up and sharing its needs.

 What Your Parts Have to Say
Being with a part that at times you may try desperately to avoid is incredibly brave, as well as fundamental to healing from suicidality. At times, these parts hold the key to healing and understanding our reactions to present and past experiences. Our parts understand more than we give them credit for, and learning to respect and support them helps us become a more holistic version of ourselves. With this in mind, try to remain curious about your suicidal part as you continue reading this book. Pay attention to that part's reactions to the new things you learn.

In the next section, we will explore avenues for healing from suicidal ideation that include the power of attending to the physical body, brain, and breath through complementary and alternative modalities. You will learn methods for reducing distress in real time to help you along your healing journey. We will also explore how many of these treatment methods were an important part of how Gina overcame her worst moments of suicidal ideation, which has led her to finally feeling more connected and balanced in her body, mind, and spirit.

 ALTERNATIVES

Healing from suicidal ideation looks different for everyone, but one thing is universal—those who have contemplated suicide have a desire not to suffer. At times, psychological and pharmacological interventions may be appropriate; however, alternative, adjunctive, and complementary approaches can offer accessible, lower-cost, additive benefits to therapy and medications. Complementary and alternative medicines (CAMs) are methods Gina used when overcoming trauma and suicidal ideation, including massage, cold plunges, breathwork, acupuncture, tai chi, and even something as simple as drinking green tea. If something is complementary, it is done in conjunction with other care (such as psychotherapy), whereas if it is alternative, it is in lieu of it. One of the most powerful parts of CAM therapies is that it places the person receiving care in the driver's seat, allowing for autonomy and self-empowerment. Some of the treatments are even self-led, meaning you get to be the master of your own healing.

In this section, we will explore commonly used and research-supported CAM therapies that help improve mental health symptoms, as well as survival rates, for those struggling with suicidality. All forms of alternative therapies rely on the power of healing and change, especially when it comes to the way we think and experience the mind, body, and spirit. Much of what CAM therapies rely on is the ability for your brain to change old, unhealthy patterns into pathways that support your desire to live and do so joyfully.

 ## Honoring My Desire to Seek Alternatives

During my work with Dr. Stirling, he helped me identify and explore my patterns and wounds to address their impact on my everyday life and relationships. We discovered my wound of abandonment, which caused me to worry about what others thought of me out of fear of being judged or left behind. This thought pattern felt like a self-imposed prison that stopped me from moving forward with things I truly wished for (such as a good relationship with a balanced life partner, confidence to pursue a career I was excited about, and love for and joyful acceptance of all parts of me).

Beyond my time in therapy, Dr. Stirling encouraged me to find things I enjoyed to fill my idle time. With his encouragement, I dove headfirst into spirituality, alternative healing practices, astrology, energy theories, religion, and meditation practices. None of my friends or family embraced these interests, and I feared being the person doing these "wacky" things outside of the circle. Because of my concern about being judged or criticized, I spent a long time searching for and attending these alternative practices in secret. Finally ready to follow my passions, I found a meditation college in Santa Monica, California, where I would do my most profound work. These classes met for four hours, three times a week in the evenings. Here, they taught the principles of being clairvoyant (having the power of seeing objects or actions beyond the range of natural vision), clairaudient (a form of extra-sensory perception wherein a person acquires information by paranormal auditory means), and clairsentient (the ability to perceive emotional or psychic energy that is imperceptible to the five standard senses) to understand myself and others. I am, admittedly, a full-fledged empath and I process any and all energy around me quickly and a lot of the times physically. Each person has a different kind of sensitivity to energy and learning about yours is a part of the fun. I found it important to sit in chairs, face to face with people who also wanted to learn about energy and to practice on each other. When I went to these classes and performed healings and readings for people I felt a great sense accomplishment. It's important to find your community through mutual interests. It you like drums, find a drum circle! I suggest getting out in the real world and not staying isolated or online. There is no replacement for in-person experiences. Building a like-minded community for support while you are healing is invaluable.

Through this consistent work and these teachings of energy principles, I saw the most significant shifts in my thoughts about suicide. My fearful ideas around suicide were replaced with appreciation for my beautiful inner light, and I diligently prioritized being loving toward myself, which I could then extend to people and animals. The more I paid attention to my energy, the more grounded I felt and the less anxiety I felt buzzing around me. I was able to find and embody a sense of calm for the first time in a long time. Committing to weekly practice ensured I was showing up for myself. In Chapter 6: Exploring Spirituality, I will share more specific teachings of the energy flow work I learned and how it reshaped my suicidal thoughts. The gist of these teachings is that when suicidal thoughts arise, you learn processes to more easily change the narrative and replace them with uplifting messages.

A Selection of Alternative Modalities
Brainwork

For better or worse, our thoughts are powerful abstract impressions that shape our reality in relation to the world around us. When these thoughts are compassionate and centered around healing and hope, suicidal thoughts have little space to exist, but when thoughts become fixated on anguish, pain, and suffering, neural pathways for suicidality are more hospitable.

So, what exactly are these pathways and why does it matter when overcoming suicidal thoughts? One way to think of it is much like a groove on a record. The more the song (or thought) is played, the deeper it becomes. The needle (or neural pathway) falls more easily into a deep groove, and so too do our thoughts. If these thoughts are of suicide, it will be more likely that our minds go there in times of pain, stress, and/or trauma. These neural circuits, which are groups of nerve fibers that carry information throughout the body via the central nervous system, make up various pathways responsible for thought and movement and even for automatic actions such as digestion and sleep. These same pathways contribute to how suicidal thoughts can become habitual. In fact, suicidal thoughts cause significant hormonal fluctuations in the brain, including serotonin abnormalities, leading to mental and physical fatigue; thinking patterns shift toward short-term thinking, and impulse control is inhibited.

According to the Center of Neuroscience at the University of California in Davis,[39] anytime we learn something new, our brains fuse unique pathways at a rapid pace (literally within seconds), meaning our brains possess plasticity and can change at any point, not just in early childhood as was once believed. No matter how long you have struggled, you have the potential to grow, even if it takes time and patience.

A powerful alternative brain therapy gaining traction in treating depression, anxiety, and trauma (which are all linked to suicidality) is neurofeedback. This noninvasive treatment, which involves placing electrodes on the scalp and then providing instantaneous feedback about the brain's activity (usually while watching television), encourages

39. Kimberly McAllister, "Making and Breaking Connections in the Brain," University of California, Davis, accessed August 21, 2023, https://neuroscience.ucdavis.edu/news/making-and-breaking-connections-brain.

the brain to develop healthy patterns of activity through the use of electroencephalography (EEG) tracking and modulation. Research shows neurofeedback has the potential to alter pervasive negative self-thoughts and nervous system dysregulation, which are known risk factors of the chronic depression that often leads to suicidal thoughts. Reducing the need for depression medication helps improve survival rates from suicide, as many of these drugs carry potential side effects that include suicidal thoughts. Finding a neurofeedback provider in your area can be as easy as searching online, and most offices provide a free consultation and initial brain scan. Much needs to be done in the way of research and support by insurance companies, so unfortunately this treatment is not financially feasible for all.

Another option for using neurofeedback to address suicidal thoughts, depression, focus, and stress management is using a product such as the Muse Brain Sensing Headband. This product is a meditation tracker and multisensor headset monitor with responsive sound feedback that helps guide you in healthy brain, heart, and breath activity. There is a free app to download with a variety of soundscapes to listen to during each session, as well as a reading of brain waves measuring how often you were able to remain focused and calm. With my own clients who use this device, they find that as little as ten minutes a day makes a significant difference in their depression symptoms, with the most benefit coming from consistency. While you can't target specific areas of the brain like a medical provider, the healing benefits are still significant and can make a dramatic impact on strengthening neural circuitries in the brain that help you feel centered, calm, and joyful. ♥

The spiritual world unites with the physical world in the human being. Consequently the spiritual world flows into the physical world in such a tangible way in us that we can sense it if we simply pay attention. —Emanuel Swedenborg, Secrets of Heaven 6057:3

Taking the Plunge

Learning about energy pathways in and around my body helped me understand how trauma was stuck in my mind and inside my body. I often found meditation helpful in moving this energy. Still, sometimes, the physical sensations were so intense that I needed ways to "touch" the pain, which motivated me to seek alternative approaches to reset my system and move energy that was not serving me. During my most severe ideation cycles, in **Phase 3: Despair** and **Phase 4: Intent,** I felt stagnant and would lie around for hours, staring into the abyss, wishing my life was different. Even when the last thing I wanted to do was move, I firmly believe connecting with my body through movement often brought me immediate relief from suicidal thoughts and despair.

Whenever I felt lethargic, I stood up, went outside, walked around my garden, and got my hands in the soil. As I moved, no matter how slowly, I felt my body return to life. I closed my eyes and felt the sun or moonlight on my face while taking a deep breath and imagining the air entering my physical space. Sometimes, I used the EFT Tapping Exercise that we will review later in this chapter because I could do it anywhere.

While these gentle walks supported me, I sometimes needed more robust physical support, which included working with more extreme hot and cold sensations. I sought sessions run by authorized trainers in each category to guide me in these more extreme body practices.

When I came across cold therapies, specifically the Wim Hof Method (which is taught by certified teachers worldwide), I felt I had found a path out of my physical anguish.

I attended a three-hour fundamentals workshop. With a background as a hospice nurse, the instructor taught the medical benefits of Wim Hof in a way that fascinated me, covering the science, uses, safety precautions, and breathing practices and, finally, guiding us to sit inside an ice bath for two full minutes. The science intrigued me, and the physical experience was transformative. I learned that focusing on relaxing my body and mind despite the physical pain from sitting in an ice bath helped improve the mental pain I was feeling while also providing me with a welcome increase in dopamine throughout my body.

The breathwork used during the plunge helped me push the tensions from deep inside me up and toward the outside of my being. I felt extreme emotions bubble to the surface as this deep tension was released. I pulled my instructor aside before my first plunge because considerable fear and memories surfaced from my experience as a young child. My parents didn't have much money, and as mentioned before, whenever I had a fever they would put me in an ice bath, which always terrified me and felt like torture. Since then, I have avoided the cold as much as possible—even in choosing where I would live. Now, I was expected again to sit in ice water for two minutes! Fear coursed through my body, but I persevered. I placed my feet and legs into the ice tub and felt an instant shock shoot through my body. My instructor locked her compassionate gaze on me as I lowered myself in with a gasp, clasping my hands. I didn't move for two entire minutes. She watched the clock as those traumatic memories surged into my mind. I felt like I was that helpless girl in the ice bath again. My face scrunched up as tight as possible, and I cried, "I don't want to!"

My instructor looked deeply at me with her chestnut-brown eyes and said, "You're doing great; breathe; I am right here." I will never forget her eyes because I felt a motherly love radiating from her, and I received it. At that moment, I connected with a sense of self-compassion and understood my strength and that I could finally release these negative childhood memories. It was like an internal sonic boom. I joined my adult self with that little girl and chose to love her unconditionally. I told her everything would be okay. When I rose up out of the tub I felt invincible, enlightened, freed, and calm. I decided that if I could sit in an ice bath and feel all those things, I could love myself enough to stay alive and use these tools to heal myself further. Biological extremes in a low dose and duration, along with breathwork, elicited some of my known triggers in a safe space so I could release them with guiding trainers. I follow this practice as needed, doing the breathwork and pulling the cold lever at the end of my showers to let it run over me for two minutes. I don't want to do it, but I know it will wake my physical body, bringing me into the present. ♥

 ### Caring for the Body

When exploring overcoming suicidality, many think about thoughts and ideas, but not often enough do we reference the suicidal body. Separating the mind from the body is not only impossible but it truly does not respect the holistic nature of a person. This is why understanding what your body feels like at times you are experiencing suicidal thoughts is crucial for coping with and caring for yourself when they arise.

Clients I work with express a wide range of physical sensations connected to suicidal thoughts—from physical pain, exhaustion, panic, and tightness in their heart center to, finally, a generalized numbness.

CARING FOR THE BODY JOURNAL PROMPT

Reflecting on your own experience, take a moment to think about a time that you were struggling with suicidal thoughts. In the space below, journal about how your body felt at the time:

_____

_____

_____

_____

_____

A common emotion related to suicidal thinking is anxiety, which manifests physically as tension or restlessness, shortness of breath, sweating, trembling, feeling weak or tired, and a fuzzy-headed feeling. Recognizing that a suicidal body can feel similar is helpful when finding alternative therapies that bring physical relief as quickly as possible. One of these alternative therapies which Gina mentioned using has been gaining recent traction. In *The History of Cold Water Immersion: A Timeline*,[40] Adam Dennison accounts that cold water immersion therapy, otherwise known as cold plunging dates back to ancient Rome.

Cold plunging has become a health trend that is proving very beneficial for improving people's physical and mental health. Research cited in Psychology Today's article, "A Cold Splash–Hydrotherapy for Depression and Anxiety"[41] has shown that cold plunging can boost your mood and help eliminate anxiety. It works to correct hormonal imbalances that contribute to depression, which is pivotal when overcoming suicidal ideation. It has also been said that cold plunging helps reset the mind, which, considering that the later phases of suicidality, specifically **Phase 4: Intent** and **Phase 5: Action**, are when more drastic choices are made, cold plunging could mean choosing to live.

While there are various ways to use this alternative therapy, the following steps can be undertaken to create a DIY ice bath at home. Make sure to check with your medical provider before proceeding.

DIY Ice Bath at Home

Step 1: Set aside post-bath towels, robes, or clothing.

Step 2: Fill a tub with cold water; then, slowly add ice, making the water as cold as you can tolerate. If you are a beginner or have low cold tolerance, set yourself up for success by starting at around 55–60°F.

Step 3: Set a timer for two to three minutes to get the benefits, never exceeding five minutes.

Step 4: Enter the ice bath while taking a few slow, controlled breaths through your nose. Enter the tub entirely on an exhale (as our exhale helps relax the nervous system).

40. Adam Dennison, "The History of Cold Water Immersion: A Timeline," *Cold Plunge Facts*, 2023, https://coldplungefacts.com/cold-water-immersion-history.
41. Peter Bongiorno, "A Cold Splash–Hydrotherapy for Depression and Anxiety," *Psychology Today*, July 6, 2014, https://www.psychologytoday.com/us/blog/inner-source/201407/cold-splash-hydrotherapy-depression-and-anxiety.

Step 5: Focus on relaxing your breath. Once in the tub, you'll notice an immediate shock to your system. This is a good thing as it is the ultimate goal. Your breathing will likely be shallow at first—work to regain control of the breath. The goal is to get your breath cycle to five to eight per minute.

Step 6: After the timer goes off, exit the bath and warm up. Dry yourself with a towel and get into warm clothing. You might consider doing some jumping jacks or bodyweight movements for five to ten minutes to regulate your temperature.

Step 7: Consider journaling about your experience or noting how your suicidal thoughts or mood were impacted.

_____

_____

_____

_____

If you are unable to practice cold plunging or do not desire to do so, you can also opt for using cold exposure in your shower like Gina does, which can be helpful if you are under stress or simply want to improve your mood. Try dropping the temperature as low as possible and attempt to relax your body for at least thirty to sixty seconds, working your way up to two to three minutes.

To enhance the experience, you can try the Wim Hof Method[42] of breathing, which they claim improves anxiety and can also be done out of the cold shower:

1. Relax your body (in any comfortable position).

2. Inhale deeply into your nose or mouth, filling your belly and chest.

3. Exhale through the mouth, then immediately breathe in again.

42. Wim Hof and Koen De Jong, *The Way of the Iceman: How the Wim Hof Method Creates Radiant, Long-term Health—Using the Science and Secrets of Breath Control, Cold-training and Commitment* (Dragon Door Publications, 2017).

4. Continue with thirty to forty short breaths in short bursts (your stomach will appear as if it is pumping in and out).

5. Take one final deep inhalation and then let the air out and stop inhaling; hold your breath until you feel the urge to breathe again.

6. Inhale very deeply to full capacity and hold for fifteen seconds; then let it go. This completes the first round.

7. Repeat the entire process, steps two through six, at least three to four times.

8. Once completed, take time to meditate and enjoy the state of deep relaxation.

EFT Tapping

Another alternative, self-administered therapy that Gina uses to support herself through distress is the emotional freedom technique, otherwise known as EFT tapping. EFT is a mind–body method of tapping acupressure points on the hands, face, and body with your fingertips, while focusing on any issue or feeling you're trying to overcome. This can be especially helpful for working through suicidal thoughts, no matter your phase of suicidality. Studies reported by the National Library of Medicine has shown that EFT helps reduce stress and anxiety, reduce cravings, and help resolve fears and insecurities.[43]

EFT Tapping Exercise

To practice this technique, reference the diagram that follows to locate the different points. Begin at point #1, the Karate Chop, then move sequentially to the last point, tapping firmly and vigorously while saying the following phrase:

"Even though I'm struggling with_____, I still love and accept myself."

---

43. Donna Bach et al. "Clinical EFT (Emotional Freedom Techniques) Improves Multiple Physiological Markers of Health," *Journal of Evidence-based Integrative Medicine* 24 (2019): 2515690X18823691.

Or,

"Even though I feel _____, I still love and accept myself."

It may not be easy to fully believe the statement at first, but it is important to try. You can change the phrasing to whatever feels authentic to you, and as you go through the points, you may desire to speak different truths to yourself. Because our voice has the power to move energy and has the ability to help us connect with ourselves and regulate our nervous system, saying the phrasing out loud adds to the healing potential of this coping skill.

Now that you've given this a try, the possibilities are endless. Some of my clients find tapping on their favorite acupressure point in times of stress, even without doing the entire pattern, to be very soothing. Some of them say they will do this when they're stuck in traffic or dealing with a conflict, while others will do it specifically to overcome thoughts of self-harm or suicide.

The Power of Breath

> "You cannot breathe in the past, you cannot breathe in the future, you can only breathe in the present." —Unknown

Our breath grounds us in the here and now and is one of the most powerful ways to work through suicidal thoughts. The rhythm in which we breathe sends signals to our brain about our perception of reality, as well as our emotional state. When our breath becomes labored, short, or shallow, our brain and body perceive that we are in a state of panic or crisis. Even if you were not feeling anxious or stressed before, poor breath quality can lead you there. While certain breathing exercises use forceful breathing to challenge the body, such as the kapalabhati pranayama (breath of fire) in Yoga, this state of labored breathing is meant to be incremental because breathing this way long-term can have negative side effects.

Pause and take a moment to check in with your breath as it is right now. How would you describe it? Smooth? Relaxed? Or is it shallow

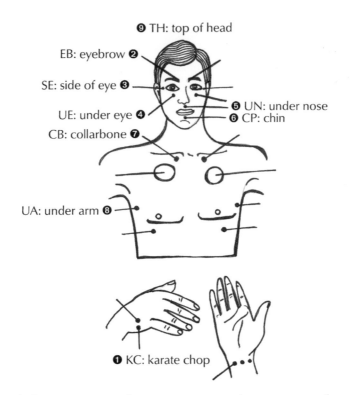

❾ TH: top of head

EB: eyebrow ❷

SE: side of eye ❸

UE: under eye ❹

CB: collarbone ❼

❺ UN: under nose
❻ CP: chin

UA: under arm ❽

❶ KC: karate chop

and tense? As we age, endure trauma, and are exposed to stress, our breath hygiene suffers. Common symptoms of poor breath hygiene include chest and throat tightness, chest pain or pain around the breastbone, and more propensity toward colds or flu, anxiety, and poor sleep quality.

This is why it is so important to practice intentional breathing every single day we are alive and especially when going through the journey of healing and overcoming suicidal ideation. While checking in on your breath right now is important, it is equally important to check in if you are experiencing suicidal thoughts or plans to hurt yourself. Being aware of the physical symptoms present during suicidal thoughts, which includes your breath, can be a powerful way to signal when you need to do grounding skills before it becomes too late.

The vagus nerve should also be taken into consideration when considering what poor breath quality does to the body. The vagus nerve begins at the nape of the neck and extends to multiple organs in the body. According to the polyvagal theory, coined by Dr. Stephen

Porges,[44] the vagus nerve sends signals to our body letting it know whether we are safe. A hallmark of extreme suicidal thoughts is that the body seems to disconnect or appear to leave the present, leading to imbalanced energy, thoughts, or for some, the feeling of impending doom or danger. Using your breath to balance and properly tone your vagus nerve can help improve stress, digestion, and sleep, as well as balance hormones, relax tension in your muscles, and help center your thoughts. This kind of practice connects you with your mental and spiritual state, allowing you to use the tools you are learning in this book.

On your journey, it is important to notice when your breath is not well regulated. When beginning breathing exercises, some people may experience dizziness or feelings of discomfort, and if at any point while practicing you feel this way, take a moment and return to your regular breathing. With practice, your body increases its ability to process CO_2 and properly use oxygen to help nourish all parts of your body.

To get started, you can try something very simple called the 4-7-8 breath. This technique is simple and powerful in combating anxiety and suicidal thoughts right in the moment. To complete this breath exercise, follow the steps below.

4-7-8 BREATHING EXERCISE
Healthy breath techniques should not be an alternative to medical interventions, but they can certainly be complementary, and the more you do them the better. Make sure not to wait until you are feeling the most extreme levels of suicidal ideation before using your chosen breath technique. As you practice, your body naturally heals and reconnects with what it knows how to do. We recommend practicing at least daily, for anywhere from one to five minutes. Setting a gentle reminder alarm on your phone can be helpful when getting started with this healing practice. With time, you will likely find your body

44. Stephen W. Porges, *The Pocket Guide to Polyvagal Theory: The Transformative Power of Feeling Safe*, First edition, New York: W. W Norton & Company, 2017.

4–7–8 Breathing

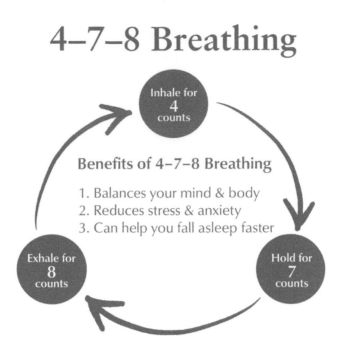

Inhale for 4 counts

Benefits of 4–7–8 Breathing

1. Balances your mind & body
2. Reduces stress & anxiety
3. Can help you fall asleep faster

Exhale for 8 counts

Hold for 7 counts

reaches for the breath it needs more naturally without having to set a reminder. Of all the complementary alternative therapies, this is one you have at your disposal anytime, anywhere.

> *The human spirit is breathing within the body.* —*Emanuel Swedenborg*, Divine Love and Wisdom 391

BREATHWORK WITH THE BODY AND SPIRIT

Whenever I was suicidal, I was extraordinarily disconnected from everything. It felt like I was living in both past and future thoughts but never in the present. At times, I was so numb I barely felt like I had a body. My soul and spirit felt ungrounded and far away. When this feeling arose, I found that working with my breath was the fastest, easiest, and most effective way to connect energetically, helping me move past challenging moments, suicidal ideation, and stuck energy. Our breath, made of fantastic life-sustaining particles, flows through our nose and mouth, down our throats and into our lungs, providing oxygen for our blood, muscles, bones, nerves, and organs. It truly is our life-force energy.

Finding the right breathwork for me was imperative, since many kinds of breath practices are available, each with different effects and benefits. Breathwork is magical when trying to connect deeply with our minds, bodies, souls, and spirits. Working with your breath intentionally puts you in the driver's seat of your life. Although your spirit is never genuinely separated from you, when you are in a low vibration (negative energy), your breath may become more shallow or short, and the quality will suffer. Doing breathwork dismantles the lower vibrational thoughts and energy (i.e., anger, fear, resentment, shame, regret, jealousy, trauma, irritability, anxiety, sadness, and loneliness). As the lower vibrations fall away, a higher life-force energy, your birthright, will allow you to connect more with your body and spirit.

As you breathe and become more connected, you elevate into a higher energy vibration (i.e., happiness, love, kindness, laughter, gratitude, compassion, excitement, joy, and glee). These positive vibrations enhance your will to live. When you feel more connected to yourself, it is less likely you will experience suicidal thoughts, or if you do, they will become much more manageable.

Receiving Alternative Healing from Others

I am always seeking more resonant modalities, practitioners, and techniques to guide me into a more profound connection with myself. I will never stop trying new things and seeking support in healing from others. I genuinely believe that acupuncture, massage, and herbal remedies from a licensed practitioner were integral in my ability to recover from suicidal ideation. Acupuncture made me feel like I was giving myself a quiet space to move energy naturally. Because many other therapies took effort, finding treatments that provided healing in a state of rest was necessary. While acupuncture may not be for everyone, it helped me show up for myself. I appreciate that acupuncture views the whole person physically and emotionally. In my acupuncture sessions, I sometimes would cry and feel the energy move and release throughout my body. Recent legislative changes have led to acupuncture being covered by certain medical plans, making this form of treatment more accessible and affordable for many.

To support my treatment, I also took a formulated herbal remedy that helped calm my nerves but did not make me drowsy. Those who take prescribed medications can also greatly benefit from supplementing with these holistic techniques; just make sure that you always check in with your medical provider before beginning any supplement or homeopathic remedies. It is also helpful to have your medical provider check your vitamin D and iron levels to assess whether you need supplementation in order to provide relief from the depressive symptoms, lethargy, or irritability that are commonly felt when suicidal.

Massage is another form of bodywork that helped me heal. Working with a trained and licensed massage therapist helped me feel safe as I worked through the stress in my physical body. I scheduled body therapies regularly to help me through some of my darkest times. For some, massage can be expensive, so it can help to find affordable options for receiving this powerful form of self-care. One option is checking with your insurance company as some medical massages may be covered through your plan; another option is to search for local massage schools that offer free or reduced pricing on services (though these students may not be trained in working with people who have undergone trauma). While there are many forms of physical massage, some of my favorites include Thai and deep tissue. Both helped me process the trauma stored in my body and mind. There are also specially trained massage therapists who offer approaches such as Emotional Trauma Release, which is a therapeutic procedure that uses craniosacral therapy to free the body and mind of the discomforting side effects of trauma. Whichever style feels right for you, know you deserve to be cared for while healing from suicidal thoughts, and alternative body therapies can be an excellent way to receive this care.

New forms of alternative medical treatments are being more closely researched, including options such as ketamine, psilocybin, and CBD.

A quick Internet search in these areas will provide you additional information and guidance since these treatments are subject to local and federal laws.

Listed below are a few other forms of healing that I've enjoyed. Some of these practices require certifications, whereas others do not. Please do diligent research and interviews in seeking practitioners in any category. In the Resource Guide (on page 212) we list several recommendations.

Bio-Tuning, Theta Healing, Sound Baths with Crystal Bowls
These therapies use specific sounds and frequencies to help balance the brain and nervous system.

Craniosacral Therapy/Hands-on Healing
A gentle, noninvasive, hands-on treatment that manipulates the joints in the cranium and is typically used by osteopaths, chiropractors, and massage therapists.

Hypnotherapy
Mind–body intervention, where hypnosis creates a state of focus and specific attention on areas the person wants to investigate.

Qigong and Tai Chi
Mind–body exercises that use meditation, breathing, and movement to increase energy and reduce stress.

Shamanic Energy Healing or Journeys with Plant Medicine
Practitioners in various categories are usually connected to the energy of natural medicines.

Finding Your Alternatives

One of the wonderful things about alternative and complementary therapies is that there is no limit to what you can try. Whether it be finding comfort through your own breath and touch, learning ways to boost your immune system and physical health, diving into energetic work as Gina did, finding a body worker who provides you comfort, learning how to rewire your own brain, or receiving the ancient practice of acupuncture, one thing is true—you can heal from suicidal ideation. Most often, for those who struggle with suicidality, something in their lives has felt out of control. Whether it be past trauma, current life stressors, chronic pain, debt, or failing relationships, how you choose to heal yourself is holistically yours to own.

As you explore alternative ways to heal, allow yourself the time and patience to see if something works. It can feel frustrating when relief does not come quickly. Remember that it took time to build the experiences and narratives that lead to suicidal thoughts; it will take consistency to heal these wounds. We also want to stress that the strategies explored in this chapter are not intended to replace any medication or medical interventions that have been working for you; instead, they can complement those therapies. However, if you have become frustrated with current interventions, you can check with your medical provider to see if some of these alternatives might work for you. The key here is to think creatively; allow yourself to explore and give yourself the grace to experiment and try new things.♥

TECHNIQUES FOR YOUR TOOLBOX

At this point in your journey, you have learned evidence-based therapies for addressing suicidal ideation, as well as a number of alternative modalities that can support your healing journey. In the remaining section, we will offer a collection of beneficial techniques you can use any time you need help navigating the uncertain terrain of healing.

Urge Surfing

Urge surfing was developed by Dr. Alan Marlatt[45] in the early 1980s as a means to help his clients treat addictive or obsessive behaviors with mindful-based relapse prevention. Instead of meeting the urges with shame, you understand them and recognize that they have phases that too shall pass. This allows for mindful awareness of thoughts and feelings without completely internalizing them. Urge surfing is a

---

45. Sarah Bowen, Neha Chawla, Joel Grow, and G. Alan Marlatt, *Mindfulness-based Relapse Prevention for Addictive Behaviors* (New York: Guilford Publications, 2011).

powerful mindfulness skill that can also be used to cope with suicidal thoughts as they arise. It involves observing an urge (for example, suicidal urges, or for someone leaving an unhealthy relationship, the urge to reach out to your ex) without taking any action (such as self-harm, substance abuse, or other coping skills to remove the pain) and then allowing the urge to subside in its own time. The skill can also be applied to breaking unhealthy habits, which serves as another protective factor since, as we explored, substance use can be a risk factor for suicidality.

Using the distress scale (SUDS), with 10 being the most distress and 0 being the least, you can use numbers to determine where you are in the wave, or you can choose to remain aware of sensations or tension in your body.

As you wait for the urge to pass, use your breath as a safety raft to help you ride the wave. Research has shown that each time you ride a wave and do not give in, the next wave is typically smaller and easier to manage. Give yourself time and patience to implement urge surfing. As you practice, it will become easier and more natural. ♈

Surfing the Peaks and Valleys
In my work with Dr. Stirling, we used the urge surfing technique. When I experienced a trauma trigger and my chest and heart ached, he would encourage me to be present with the sensations. The ache would expand throughout my body, where I would "peak" in a full-body

episode of anxiety around a traumatic memory. Witnessing this peak, without trying to run from it, helped me understand that these sensations were part of the process. No matter how horrible I felt, there would be an end to the pain, which reassured me that I could get through it. If it got really hard, I would go to my toolbox of meditations or things that helped settle me, and soon, the event would "fall" off. Using this skill continues to help me regain my place in the driver's seat of my life. Knowing that suffering is a normal part of life and that pain and urges ebb and flow has been integral to my healing process.

When considering urge surfing and my suicidal ideation, I noticed that my episodes would pass faster, and the intensity of the thoughts seemed more manageable because I could recall other times they had passed. I remember once I received an email from a friend who wanted to leave our friendship. It came out of the blue; I had thought we were close. She explained that my constant focus on working on myself made her anxious and that she preferred having friends with less complicated lives. Her words hit me like a train of pain, and I cried deeply. I began contemplating again about why I was alive as my abandonment wounds came flooding in. I wrote her a card that said, "Sorry, what can I do?" and sent flowers and a bottle of wine.

I didn't understand that she was setting boundaries for the life she wanted. This wave of pain and the urge to hurt myself took days to peak as layers of fear and sadness moved through me. Despite all of this, I still knew it would eventually taper off, and it did. As I waited, I threw myself into practices of self-love and care. I took long baths, meditated, hiked in the sunshine, sat on the beach, and spent as much time as possible in nature. I was able to get to a place where I could see the situation from a healthier perspective, all without hurting myself. I realized that neither of us were wrong in the situation. Without urge surfing or using my tools, I would have internalized blame and convinced myself that I either had to fix the relationship or did not deserve to be alive. Instead, I learned that knowing someone's truth was better than pretending we were meant to remain friends. It allowed me space to focus on the relationships that did work. Without waiting for the urges and pain to subside, I believe I may not have been around to see the joy and beauty that comes after. ♡

> *Neither time and the passage of time nor space and extension in space can be used to describe our inner depths, or our feelings and the thoughts they produce. They do not exist in time or in a place, even though they seem to do so, as far as our worldly senses can tell. Rather they exist in inner dimensions corresponding to time and place. These corresponding dimensions can only be called states; there is no other word for them. It is called a change of state in our inner depths when we have a change of mind or heart, or a change in our feelings and the thoughts they produce, from sad to happy, from happy back to sad, from godless to godly or devout, and so on. These changes are called changes in state. They have to do with our feelings, and to the extent that our feelings control our thoughts, with our thoughts as well.* —Emanuel Swedenborg, Secrets of Heaven 4850

Boundary Setting for Empaths and Highly Sensitive Persons

Taking time to direct love inward is an important part of healing from suicidal ideation, and it is especially important for people who are empaths or highly sensitive persons (HSPs). HSPs are neurodivergent individuals (someone whose brain processes information in a way that is not typical of most individuals but comes with its own strengths and challenges) who have increased activity in their central nervous system and are more sensitive to physical, emotional, or social stimuli. In addition to being more sensitive to stress, a survey of 326 HSPs conducted by psychotherapist and HSP[46] specialist Julie Bjelland showed:

---

46. Julie Bjelland, "Are Highly Sensitive People More Susceptible to Suicide? Survey Results Including Recommended Resources," January 20, 2023, https://www.juliebjelland.com/hsp-blog/are-highly-sensitive-people-more-susceptible-to-suicide-survey-results-including-recommended-resources.

- 90.2 percent of HSPs have had thoughts of suicide;
- 18.4 percent have attempted suicide;
- 32.8 percent use alcohol or drugs to numb emotional pain.

The increased risk for suicidal thoughts in HSPs is not necessarily that they encounter more suffering but rather, that when they encounter suffering, it impacts them more significantly. Coping with not only personal pain but the pain experienced by others in the world can be overwhelming. Other risk factors include managing sensory overload and not knowing how to get the support or empathy needed for your sensitivity.

Highly Sensitive Person Self-Assessment

To find out if you are an HSP, respond to the following statements. For each statement check "yes" whether you feel this way some/most of the time:

HSP Statements	YES
Sensory input from my environment overwhelms me (bright lights, strong smells, coarse fabrics, loud noises).	
I am impacted by the mood and energy of those around me.	
I am sensitive to physical pain or discomfort.	
I pick up on subtleties in my environment (i.e., clutter or well-balanced spaces).	
I need to withdraw on busy days—sometimes to a dark room, my bed, or simply to be alone.	
I am deeply conscientious.	
I am deeply moved by music and art.	

HSP Statements	YES
I am particularly impacted by caffeine (either sensitive to it or experience extreme withdrawal when I do not have it).	
My nervous system sometimes makes me feel agitated—especially when tired.	
I have a strong startle response.	
Having a lot to do at once overwhelms me.	
Being under time pressure is distressing to me.	
I tend to know what needs to be done to make people more comfortable in their environment (like changing the lighting or temperature of a room).	
I am sensitive to the effects of medication and drugs.	
I do not tend to enjoy violent movies or TV shows.	
I find change to be difficult.	
Hunger strongly disrupts my concentration or mood.	
I notice and enjoy pleasant scents, tastes, sounds, and works of art.	
When I compete or am observed (perhaps at work) while performing a task, I become nervous or shaky, causing me to perform worse than I would otherwise.	
I make a lot of effort to avoid mistakes or forgetting things.	
As a child, adults around me considered me to be sensitive or shy (even if at a very young age).	
I make a lot of effort to avoid upsetting or overwhelming situations.	
I am annoyed when people try to get me to do too many things at once.	

Scoring

If you answered more than thirteen of the questions as "yes," you are likely a highly sensitive person. This information is meant to encourage further exploration as no person can be described holistically in one single survey.

According to Dr. Elaine Aron,[47] one of the founding researchers on the topic, having fewer questions which feel extremely true might also indicate high sensitivity; and furthermore, she has found that men and women are equally highly sensitive, though men tend to answer fewer items as true, which is likely due to societal expectations around masculinity.

As was explored in the **5 Phases of Healing from Suicidality**, investing time and energy in yourself is important for everyone but especially for empaths and HSPs. Though HSPs are more susceptible to the pain in the world, they are also more positively influenced by its beauty. They also tend to receive more benefit from healing practices such as therapy, yoga, spiritual work, and other modalities. For this reason, HSPs make up a larger portion of those who continue to invest in therapy as they gain a great deal from the experience, as well as from the relationships formed with their therapists. When a sensitive person is not receiving this type of support, a large void occurs, which can increase mental health issues and, for some, suicidal thoughts. Being with others who care for you and support your sensitivity improves the sense of well-being and ability to heal these issues. Often seen as emotional sponges and susceptible to their environment, HSPs must set boundaries with the people in their lives and their environments if they want to remain in a space of healing from suicidal ideation.

Boundary Setting

When setting boundaries, it is helpful to recognize the way it makes you feel both emotionally and physically. For many empaths, HSPs,

47. Elaine Aron, *The Highly Sensitive Person: How to Thrive When the World Overwhelms You* (New York: Kensington Publishing Corp., 2013).

or people pleasers, there can be a level of *unearned guilt* (feeling guilty for something you are not responsible for) associated with boundary setting. Boundary setting is beneficial not only for your healing journey but for the health of your relationships. Knowing what you need to prioritize to feel safe and loved and leaning into that is an important part of healing from suicidal ideation. If anyone makes you feel these efforts are wrong or lack meaning, it may be time to assess the role these people play in your life. In my book, *Gaslighting Recovery for Women: The Complete Guide to Recognizing Manipulation and Achieving Freedom from Emotional Abuse,*[48] I outline the use of flexible versus firm boundaries.

Flexible boundaries include acknowledging the other person's opinion and still being open to ongoing conversation. Flexible does not mean you are going to back down, but rather, it includes an open tone used when asserting yourself.

- "I respect your opinion, but I have my own as well."
- "I am sorry, but I don't have time."
- "That is not going to work for me."
- "Let me pause you right there."

Firm boundaries are used when someone has previously disregarded your needs and is not open to hearing your request for boundaries in the present. Firm boundary statements are most effective with a clear, but mindful tone.

- "I don't have time."
- "I don't want to."
- "No." (*This is a full sentence and needs no further explanation!*)
- "That is not going to work for me."

---

48. Amelia Kelley, *Gaslighting Recovery for Women: the Complete Guide to Recognizing Manipulation and Achieving Freedom from Emotional Abuse* (New York: Random House, 2023).

When considering your journey toward healing from suicidal ideation, you may need to set boundaries with unhealthy people or situations. Depending on the nature of the relationship, completely cutting someone out may not be possible. In these cases, *limiting contact* as much as possible can still be powerful. Examples of this include:

- Leaving the home more for your own healing practices, work, hobbies, relationships, etc.

- Limiting what you tell this person

- Reducing phone calls or only having virtual contact

- Not asking their opinion because, as Brené Brown said in her Netflix special, *The Call to Courage*,[49] you do not have to consider the opinions of people unwilling to get into the same ring of courage and vulnerability as you—not everyone's opinion of you matters

If you choose firm boundaries because someone is harmful for your healing journey, remember these key factors:

- Virtual contact (social media, texts) still can influence how you think and feel, and for some, "radio silence" is crucial;

- Due to the nature of a trauma bond, if you see the person, your body, mind, and spirit may likely revert to how you felt the last time you saw them; this does not mean you should remove your boundary or that you are destined to be around this person, rather it is a natural and normal response to being activated by your past;

- You have the right to change your opinion at any time; if at one point you had a relationship and eventually it is not helping you heal, you have the right to cut it off.

---

49. *The Call to Courage*, directed by Sandra Restrepo (2019; Los Gatos, CA: https://www.netflix.com/title/81010166/).

When considering your healing journey, list any relationships, situations, or things that you feel you need boundaries around and why:

_____

_____

_____

Do these boundaries need to be firm or flexible?

_____

_____

_____

How would you like to set these boundaries? For example: text, phone call, a letter, radio silence, and distance.

_____

_____

_____

If it were completely safe to do so, what would you like to say to this person?

_____

_____

_____

 ## Connecting with the Right People

Probably the most important part of healing is the willingness to open yourself up to support and knowledge from others. This is not simply to overcome the feeling of loneliness that often coincides with active suicidal ideation, but it is also imperative for living a long and vital life. Our immune systems and longevity are directly connected to fostering communities, no matter how small. Telomeres, which are structures made from DNA sequences and proteins found at the ends of chromosomes (think caps on the ends of electrical wires), are kept more intact with a healthy lifestyle and especially through socializing. Preserving the structure of these proteins is crucial for staving off things like Alzheimer's and other issues with cognitive decline as we age. In essence, people (the right ones) can serve as medicine.

Whether in the form of a healer, therapist, guru, or friend, receiving support from others and eventually extending this support to others are integral parts of healing from suicidal ideation. For many, healing one's own suffering includes helping others who can relate to our pain. This act helps create a sense of purpose from past experiences as a means to integrate past trauma. 🍃

> In the spiritual world, all union takes place by means of attentiveness. When anyone there is thinking about someone else because of a desire to talk with her or him, that other person is immediately present. They see each other face to face. The same thing happens when someone is thinking about someone else because of a loving affection, but in this case the result is a union, while in the former case it is only presence. This phenomenon is unique to the spiritual world. The reason is that everyone there is spiritual. It is different in the physical world, where all of us are material. In this physical world, the same thing is happening in the feelings and thoughts of our spirits, but since there is space in this world, while in the spiritual world there only seems to be space, the things that happen in the thoughts of our spirits come out in actions there. —Emanuel Swedenborg, Divine Providence 29

A Brief Defusion Meditation

The following meditation can be done any time you need to defuse from thoughts or emotions of others to become the observer of these thoughts, rather than internalizing and overattaching to them.

Begin by settling in; let your face soften, your shoulders drop, and your arms and legs relax.

Pause.

Find your center as you bring your attention onto the rhythm of your breath.

Next, identify a distressing thought, sensation, or experience that is currently troubling you.

Imagine yourself entering a theater and sitting comfortably in the front row.

Next, see the situation or emotions you were feeling portrayed up on the screen, much like a movie would be.

Notice the characters, the situation, and your reaction to the movie.

If you wish, you can choose to change the movie or allow the screen to go blank.

Return to your breath and reconnect with your body.

If you need more comforting, place one hand on either shoulder, much like a hug, and begin tapping left and right as your sooth your body and mind with the "butterfly hug."

When you feel more settled and ready, open your eyes and express personal gratitude for taking care of yourself.

CONCLUSION

While this chapter explored evidence-based therapies and various trailheads for self-care, the next chapter will explore another pillar of healing: spirituality. Because every individual's relationship to spirituality is very personal and at times can create cultural burdens, we found it important to offer this topic in its own autonomous space. We recognize that spirituality and religion can be part of a struggle for some when finding personal value and freedom. For Gina, spirituality was vital to her healing journey, so we share this chapter as a window into how it could be beneficial, as another trailhead to explore on your journey.

Chapter 6: Exploring Spirituality

God created us in such a way that our inner self is in the spiritual world and our outer self is in the physical world. Therefore to make us permanent and everlasting beings, God made us citizens of both worlds so that the spiritual part of us, which belongs in heaven, could be planted in the physical part belonging to this world the way a seed is planted in the ground. —*Emanuel Swedenborg,* True Christianity 14

WHEN EXPLORING HOW to overcome, heal, and survive suicidal ideation, spirituality and religiosity are some of the most common protective factors. Research shows[50] that religion often prevents suicide attempts, while the connection and practice of spirituality (with or without religion) can help prevent suicidal thoughts significantly. In much of this book, Gina has been sharing her story of what caused her ongoing thoughts of suicide and how they escalated into self-harm. The major catalyst of healing for Gina was her spiritual practice,

50. Alee Robins and Amy Fiske, "Explaining the Relation Between Religiousness and Reduced Suicidal Behavior: Social Support Rather than Specific Beliefs," *Suicide and Life-Threatening Behavior* 39, no. 4 (2009): 386-395.

and in this chapter, she will provide an in-depth exploration into the concepts and theories behind these practices. *Spirituality* is the exploration of something beyond or deemed more significant than the ego, and for this reason it remains ever-changing and evolving. At the same instance you are learning from Gina's experience, she will be continuing to do so in her own life.

In this chapter, we will explore three spiritual principles that were core to Gina's process. We will also explore the meaning and essence of the ego in our lives and how this aspect of our psyche connects to spiritual purpose. Lastly, we will introduce the system of chakras and how this helps ground our sense of spirituality in our body. We end the chapter with a guided meditation to help you connect to spirituality in your life right now in a way that is comfortable, even if this is something new for you to be exploring. ♥

GINA'S CORE SPIRITUAL PRINCIPLES
Birth

To overcome suicidal ideation, we must consider the magnitude of birthing a soul. When I was born, just like everyone else, I came in with a "soul spark." At birth, and before life's sorrows and challenges, I was anchored in the highest vibrational light from God's source, which connected me to Earth and the universe. God's source is our primary guiding teacher, the purest unconditional love vibration, and the source of all wisdom and universal information. I entered this world through my mother's soul spark, where a tiny bit of her spark broke off to create me, give me life, and animate my body. The energetic exchange between baby me and my mother was, unquestionably, miraculous. We all share the same miracle that originates from this soul spark. Understanding this spark has inspired me to help my fellow humans find and hold their own soul spark. Even the most seemingly hardened souls still have this spark; yet life can dim it to the point where it becomes difficult to see, feel, or hear anymore. To return to our light again, we need to receive support from others and from a deep connection to our own soul.

How the Soul Connects to the Body

Through my clairvoyant training, I have been a part of several classes and teachings about what people refer to as the "silver cord" that connects the body to the soul. I have experienced this firsthand in my readings and healings. Although there is no way to say this as an absolute truth, having this knowledge helped me to feel more closely connected to my spirit, and I've embraced it. What I've come to understand is that we each have a silver cord invisible to our eyes that connects our soul to our physical body. When our physical body sleeps, the soul does not; instead, it is actively continuing to learn other lessons or gain wisdom, which it sometimes shares in dreams. As we wake, that silver cord recoils back into the body. It is normal to wake up and feel disoriented because you are not fully integrated yet (in science this is referred to as the hypnagogic state). For this reason, it is important to be gentle upon waking. When you are ready, this can be a beautiful time to do healing work and practices that help you feel integrated and supported.

Dolores Cannon,[51] a contemporary spiritual teacher, hypnotherapist, past-life regressionist, and prolific author of seventeen books, also speaks about the silver cord and its connectivity. Those dealing with suicidal thoughts commonly struggle to reconnect with this cord, yet it always remains present, and engaging in spiritual practice can help them reconnect.

Understanding the soul spark and the silver cord were instrumental to my transformation and healing because they helped me sense the complex forces at play in getting and keeping my soul in this body. I now appreciate that I am not just this physical mass with a supercomputer in my head, wandering aimlessly around. Instead, my energy and life force are all around me, working with and for me. At my most suicidal I felt utterly alone, yet I never feel alone now that I have embodied this understanding. I am grateful that spiritual practice has

---

51. Dolores Cannon, *Between Death & Life: Conversations with a Spirit* (Ozark Mountain Publishing, 1993).

helped me realize that I am not outside the circle of connection, as I always have a connection to the spiritual core within me. I am proud that I have not only found myself but have also removed the shame I was carrying. Without carrying this shame, I have more energy to fight for my soul and I can't think of a better reason to fight. If I am not paying attention to my spiritual side, it will find a way to get my attention. It will begin to "tap" on my energy through messages or synchronicities, just like a bird outside of a window gently tapping with its beak, trying to get my attention: "tap, tap, tap." ☙

Death and Rebirth

In the previous section, we explored how connecting with the energy of birth can help you regain a sense of belonging and connection with the soul to reduce suicidal ideation. In this section, we focus on death and rebirth. We don't mean a physical death, but rather the spiritual part of us that wants to let go so it can continue the journey of learning, growing, and having life experiences. Letting go to continue this journey is another fundamental part of overcoming thoughts of suicide, allowing us to look at all of life's experiences, the good and the bad, as part of the growth process. Letting go allows certain aspects of our suffering to die away.

This is the reason we are all here. The birth–death–rebirth process is a cycle we must go through step by step, no matter how painful certain phases become, so we can come to recognize what we are here to learn. Leaving a situation, thought process (such as suicidality), or relationship that no longer serves our highest purpose allows for rebirth and a path forward. We are, in a way, new again—an enhanced version of ourselves with more profound wisdom and experiences. ☙

Resistance

Letting go of suicidal thoughts can be a dramatic change for some people. Often, we resist change because the unknown can be frightening. Most of us have had a life situation that we wished we could have stopped or changed. When in a space of resistance we may deny the issue and look for ways to avoid the inevitable. For example, about six months before my husband left, I felt a shift and knew I was losing him. Deep inside, I also wanted a different marriage experience, but resistance compelled me to do everything I could to stop him from leaving me. Our marriage was a contract I was determined to keep. It was my identity. I worried what people would think of me, convinced they would see me as a failure. The most challenging part was that I still loved him. Though I knew the end was coming, I resisted it. My resistance made it so much worse, and my suicidal ideation intensified into increased intent (Phase 4) and thoughts of suicidal plans and actions (Phase 5) throughout the first year of our separation.

Resistance Journal Prompt

What is something (past or present) you have adamantly resisted and how did you do so? What was that experience like? What feelings do you recall? What impact did this have on your suicidal ideation? In which suicidal phases did you find yourself? Take a moment to journal below:

_____

_____

_____

_____

_____

Resistance runs through you energetically as stagnation, creating energy blockages in your chakras. This creates a heavy, stuck feeling, which can make it more difficult to achieve rebirth. It can also cause various misalignments if it persists for long periods. When engaging in the meditation and energy work later in this chapter, you can identify where you are holding resistance and work to release it. This work is not intended to change the actual situation in your life, but rather, how your energy responds to it.

In my marriage, if I could have worked through my resistance earlier, I could have experienced a sense of rebirth more quickly, protecting me from much of my suicidal ideation. I would have seen our lives moving in two different directions and would have been able to understand that it was okay. I could have chosen to still hold love for someone even if they were no longer in my life. We are all still connected in spirit, and I look toward the future with excitement instead of fear.

The thing to remember is that rebirth always comes. Always. You have lived and learned and are constantly becoming a new version of yourself. At times, it might have hurt, bruised, or pained you, but you own all the parts of you that make up your beautiful soul spark.

> *Before we can learn what is true and be affected by what is good, the things that stand in the way and resist have to be put aside. The old self must die before the new self can be conceived.*
> —*Emanuel Swedenborg,* Secrets of Heaven 18

THE EGO'S WILL TO SURVIVE

Having a sense of who we are, our self-esteem and self-importance, is the basic premise of the ego. Research has shown[52] that higher levels of ego resiliency buffer against suicidal ideation, especially among those with more severe cases of depression or social anxiety. Engaging in insight-developing activities such as therapy, journaling, affirmations, positive self-talk, and self-reflection all engage you in different points of view and experiences that increase self-confidence and the ability to feel self-love, which are all essential for a healthy ego state. The more nourishment your ego receives, the more it has the will to live and overcome suicidal ideation. Even in the face of adversity, the ego can grow as it identifies its unique qualities and chooses to speak

52. Eun Hyun Seo, et. al., "Ego-resiliency Moderates the Risk of Depression and Social Anxiety Symptoms on Suicidal Ideation in Medical Students," *Annals of General Psychiatry* 21, no. 1 (2022): 19.

up and put self-protective plans into action, such as choosing to live instead of committing suicide.

As we have learned in the chapter thus far, spirituality plays a key role in gaining insight and exploring more profound levels of the human experience. In the following section, Gina will explore how there must be balance when focusing on the ego and an effort not to practice hyperfixation. She shares how this state of overattaching to the ego can cause further suffering and suicidal ideation. From there, the importance of purpose and meaning for a more balanced ego will be presented, as supported by Dr. Viktor Frankl's logotherapy,[53] which purports that no matter the amount of suffering, neurosis and mental health will improve when a person identifies purpose and meaning in their life.

When You Insist, Your Soul Resists

Ego, in its balanced state, is essential to human survival. The ego is robust; it gives us the drive to achieve, build, and manifest the life experiences we need to grow. Yet, the state of egomania (which is the excessive preoccupation with one's ego, identity, or self) lacks the heart-filled energy where love and compassion are found. When the ego operates in excess, its negative traits often include hurting others and can be a detriment to our civilization. This makes many people feel disconnected, especially today's youth, putting them at risk for suicidal ideation.

Common Qualities of Excess Ego Reflection Exercise

Uncompromising

Hard

Controlling

Jealous

53. Chetan Arvind Joshi, *An Empirical Validation of Viktor Frankl's Logotherapeutic Model* (University of Missouri-Kansas City, 2009).

Vindictive nature

Overly entitled

Need to "win"

In reading the list, you may have identified parts of yourself that carry these characteristics. Not feeling connected to your life purpose is a common reason people experience these issues and feel sorrowful. When you find yourself caught in negative ego expression, journal or mentally ask yourself the following questions:

- Can I stop, breathe, and do internal work before responding to this email, person, situation, or the like?

- Can I look at a situation from a different point of view? What part of my ego is this coming from?

- What is the energy around the situation?

- Is this situation triggering past trauma in me?

- Do I feel I need to be right?

- Am I operating from a place of love or fear? If the energy is from fear, can I find ways to release that energy?

- Can I bring levity to the situation and turn it into a positive?

- Can I remember their soul spark, see their life force, and remember that we are all here trying to make the best lives for ourselves?

- Can I forgive myself and them for anything we might have done?

Balanced Ego

Finding energy, direction, and support will help you identify what fills your soul. While choosing work to help support you financially is often essential for stability, it can help to listen to your intuition about what you want to do when you have time off to explore. While life stress and trauma keep us disconnected from these introspections, choosing a time or day during the week to weave exploration into your life can be helpful, especially when bringing the ego in as an ally. Some things that activate positive ego states are meditating, exercising, stretching, listening to music, physically connecting with someone you care for or love, going out in nature, volunteering, and being creative in whatever way works for you. You might even be an engineer who wants to discover a better way to use fuel; it doesn't have to be fine art.

As you weigh different options and make considerations for how to enhance your positive ego states, try asking:

What most excites me?

What might lead me toward something I would be proud of?

Focusing with this growth mindset helps lift your energy and spirit because you are learning what your soul seeks.

Some benefits you can anticipate from spiritual, energy work and letting go of the fixed ego include:

- Refined intuition
- Validating instead of trashing the self
- Feeling less worried about what others think and feeling more secure
- Less critical judgment of the self and others
- A desire and excitement to learn new things
- Improvement in health and energy levels
- Attracting kinder, more positive people, projects, and opportunities
- Ability to see and feel people's soul spark even when they are not being kind
- A deep knowing of how special you are
- Feeling grounded and lighter
- A deeper sense of gratitude
- Ability to feel healthy levels of compassion and empathy for yourself and others

- A greater sense of presence

- Living more authentically with the ability to speak up in strength, not fear

- Much more laughing, dancing, and singing from the whole body, mind, spirit, and soul

BALANCING THE CHAKRAS TO OVERCOME SUICIDAL IDEATION

Chakras are energy centers in the body that correlate to a specific region and run down the midline (or central channel) of the body, connecting the crown of the head to the root in the pelvic bowl. There are major chakras (including the seven main chakras) and minor chakras (including areas such as feet, knees, palms, ears, spleen, liver, kidneys and vagus nerve). About the size of a dollar coin, they continuously spin unless a blockage stops them from functioning, preventing any new information and energy from being stored or processed. The front of the chakra spins clockwise, and the back of the chakra spins counterclockwise. There are a variety of colors running through them, depending on the quality of the energy and where they are in the body. There are twelve rings with eleven lines and each ring can move independently. It is best if they are all running the same direction at the same time, and this might be why you have heard, "Your chakras are unbalanced."

The following is the Sanskrit name of each chakra, a basic description of where it is in the body, the color, and the self-actualization experienced when the chakra is balanced.

> **One:** Muladhara. The tailbone or base of the pelvis. Red. Self-preservation.
>
> **Two:** Svadhisthana. The sacrum. Orange. Self-gratification.
>
> **Three:** Manipura. The solar plexus. Yellow. Self-definition.
>
> **Four:** Anahata. The heart. Green. Self-love.
>
> **Five:** Vishuddha. The throat. Blue. Self-expression.

Six: Ajna. Between the eyebrows. Indigo. Self-reflection.

Seven: Sahasrara. The top of the head. Violet. Self-knowledge.

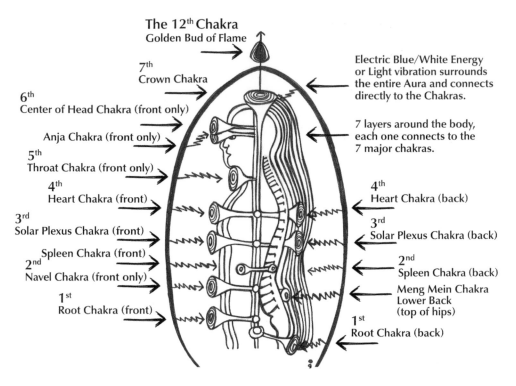

In our bodies and spirits, the colors represent the energy moving through us and communicating with our chakras. When you start to see these colors in your space as you meditate, you can focus on whichever form of self-actualization is associated with that color. For instance, if you are seeing green, you can send your energy to your heart center and focus on self-love. You can also choose to use chakra colors to help bring balance when experiencing suicidal ideation. If you are stressed or nervous, you might opt for soothing colors like green or blue, which balance the heart and throat chakras. If you're feeling depressed, you can boost your mood by wearing red, orange, or yellow to activate your root, sacral, or solar plexus chakras, helping you feel more grounded.

The reason all this work is so important for the journey of overcoming suicidal ideation is that the body of the suicidal person possesses chakras that are no longer flowing with enough energy and light. Each chakra in the major network should have energy and light feeding the next chakra. This means that the chain should not be broken, and if it is, it can cause many issues both emotionally and physically. If the chakras are not touching, such as in an acutely suicidal person who is most likely in **Phase 3: Despair** or beyond, they are most likely experiencing a loss of stability from their root chakra or perhaps a sense of powerlessness from their sacral chakra. They may feel completely disconnected from any source of energy, meaning they are not expressing enough (or potentially any) light or vibration from the crown chakra.

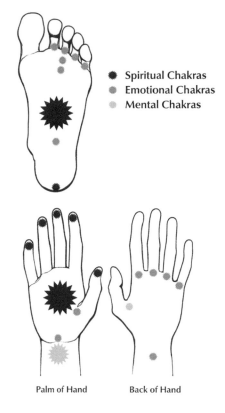

Locations of the Foot and Hand Chakras

The feeling of disconnection makes it much more challenging to overcome suicidal thoughts. While many of us think of disconnection from others as a risk factor, the chakra system shows us how we can also become disconnected from the Self. This is another example of how the energy flow that Swedenborg referenced[54] connects us to parts of ourselves but inevitably also connects us to the souls and bodies of those around us. It's how we give and experience love and how we give and experience energy. These cords for suicidal people tend to be fragile, causing them to feel even more disconnected from others. This is why consistent practice of spirituality, exploration, and chakra balancing is imperative when healing from suicidal thoughts.

54. Eleanor Mariakali Schnarr, "Door of my Heart: Comparative Internal Breathing in Yogananda and Swedenborg," June 2023, https://.spiritualquesters.org/wp-content/uploads/2023/06/Door-of-my-Heart-ODB-1.pdf.

The following meditation will integrate all the spiritual practices and principles discussed in this chapter. At the core, you will learn how to:

1. Ground yourself to the Earth and Self to release energy that no longer serves you.

2. Call back your energy with golden suns, which is meant to refill you with your most energetic life force and high vibrational energy. ♡

The Liberated Healer's "Spiritual Compass Meditation"

(20 minutes)

To realign your chakras and find liberation from suicidal ideation, try the following meditation. You can perform this practice several times daily as needed to align your energy. Because breathing directly impacts the ability to balance your chakras, we encourage you to practice conscious breathing throughout the meditation.

Step One
Posture: If you can sit in a chair with your back straight, that is preferable; if not, you may lie down. Keep your feet flat on the ground. Put your hands on your thighs with your palms facing the sky. Close your eyes. Become aware of your breath and take a few slow, deep breaths in and out until you feel some sense of calm.

Step Two
Grounding: Remaining aware of your breath, you will now practice enhanced grounding, which is essential to any spiritual work. Much like installing electricity into a building, the human body is alive with energy (electricity); we must ground our energy like an electrician, so we can manage it and move it accordingly.

How to Ground: Imagine a wide tube or tree trunk at least two inches wider than your hips. This is your grounding cord; imagine it going down through the Earth to the center where the lava is found. Imagine all the things you no longer want to hold, or all the things you want to release, going down the cord and burning away.

Step Three

About Cosmic and Earth Energy: As spiritual beings, we are divinely connected to the Earth (ground) and the universal cosmic energy. When we intentionally run our energy through these circuits, it helps flush out and align all our energy throughout our bodies, including our auras.

How to Process Earth Energy: Still grounded by the cord to the Earth's center, identify the center of each of your feet. Visualize the root (Muladhara) chakra as a round, dollar-coin-sized opening, and draw the Earth's energy into your feet; let it travel up through the legs and all the way to your hips and let it sit there for a moment as you shift to the cosmic energy circuit.

How to Process Cosmic Energy: About three inches above our head is Sahasrara, the seventh chakra, which looks like a mini round, flat-lying disc above your head. Imagine it opening and allowing energy channel to travel out past the Earth's orbit and into space, to a star or a planet. Feel the powerful cosmic energy, capture it, and bring it down through the channel to the opened seventh chakra. Imagine that the cosmic energy holds the highest vibrational color of violet. Bring the energy through the seventh chakra and let it enter the top of your head and travel down your spine to the hips, where the Earth energy is.

How to Combine the Energies: Earth energy is heavier than cosmic energy, so if you have too much Earth, it can tire you. When combining the energies, consider a balance of 10 percent Earth and 90 percent cosmic. You can say it out loud or in your mind—your Spirit knows what you mean. Let that mix in your base, and then, bring that combined energy up the front half of your body. Let the energies rise again above the seventh chakra then fall like a fountain to clean your entire aura. Let it travel down your arms and release out of your hand chakras where they are opened.

You are now running your energy using both Earth and cosmic energy!

Step Four

Using the Golden Sun Process: After draining out all the excess or stagnant energy, it is important to replenish your chakras with positive energy that is of your own essence.

How to Call Back Your Energy: Create a bubble over your head and imagine it growing with golden sunlight, holding all your original life-force energy inside. When it gets big enough, let that bubble pop, releasing the energy to fill your aura and fall around you. Repeat this as often as you wish.

> *We were created to reflect the structure of the three heavens. So the image of heaven is imprinted on us in such a perfect way that we are a miniature heaven at its smallest scale, which is why we have a correspondence with the heavens.* —Emanuel Swedenborg, Secrets of Heaven 4041

CONCLUSION

The practices in this chapter were a few of the many directions your spiritual journey can lead when overcoming suicidal ideation. For Gina, these were some of the most impactful practices that she used personally and continues to use in guiding others on their journey toward liberation and healing. The main thread through each practice—the soul spark work, birth–death–rebirth, cord connecting, ego states, and chakra balancing—was the willingness to learn and grow and expand.

As spiritual growth continues, you will likely find the **5 Phases of Suicidal Ideation** are becoming more manageable and easier to comprehend. This awareness is a sign that you are moving through the **5 Phases of Healing from Suicidality.** A fundamental aspect to healing is coming back to the tools and skills found at each trailhead as often as is needed. This will allow you to live with intention and embody the gift you are to this world. Although the healing process will look different for everyone, you can trust that when you show up and take steps on your healing journey, you are moving closer to a life of fulfillment and purpose. In Part 3: The Gift of You, we explore living in wholeness and self-compassion. ❧

The Gift of You

Chapter 7: Meaning

The inmost recesses are where heavenly joy comes from.
—*Emanuel Swedenborg,* Secrets of Heaven *545*

AT THIS POINT in the journey, you have gone through the forest of suicidal ideation and traversed the rolling landscape of healing to reach a new horizon—one of meaning and purpose, of knowing your worth and feeling whole. In this chapter, we will explore finding meaning and hope by exploring the power of forgiveness, self-worth, and overcoming doubt, as well as by using creative expression to affirm your value. All of this brings you toward "trauma integration," an important part of healing that happens when you can reflect and acknowledge the personal growth and strengths that come out of suffering. Integration of trauma allows you to determine how your personal story impacted you, rather than be a victim or bystander to your experiences. The story you tell yourself about trauma and suicidal thoughts will either tie you to these events or they can help facilitate action and change—providing meaning and depth to your life that you would not have gained otherwise

As shown in the **5 Phases of Healing** in Chapter 4, being of service to others is an important step in long-lasting healing. Whether formally through your work and deeds (much like what motivated me to become a trauma therapist and Gina to become a liberated healer and holistic practitioner) or through empathy and a heightened awareness of how to protect others from a worse fate, your pain has meaning.

Much like there are five phases of healing, so too are there **5 Phases of Forgiveness.** When you find meaning in difficult experiences, moments may come to pass when you contemplate forgiveness. Forgiveness is not intended as a gift or as a necessary action you must give to a person or group that hurts you; rather, it is an action and gift that you give to yourself. You can choose to let go of the tension, sorrow, and resentment lodged in the energy centers of your body without ever having to say a word to the person you are forgiving. Even on a physical level, harboring anger hurts your physical body. Heart rate, blood pressure, and respiration all increase when experiencing anger, along with an increase in body temperature and the stress hormone cortisol. Short periods of this are a natural part of being human, but over time it can have a negative impact on your overall health and wellness.

Forgiveness is an important part of moving toward lasting healing from suicidal ideation. Some offenses may seem impossible to forgive, and we do not suggest this is an easy journey. If needed, you can choose to let go of smaller pains that feel less intimidating to overcome. Forgiveness is a personal journey, and it is entirely up to you.

ACCESSING YOUR WHOLENESS WITH THE 5 PHASES OF FORGIVENESS

The following is a detailed description of the **5 Phases of Forgiveness** to be used during your healing journey. According to psychologists at Berkeley,[55] forgiveness is a conscious, deliberate decision to release feelings of resentment or vengeance toward a person or group who has harmed you, regardless of whether they deserve your forgiveness.

No two persons' journeys are alike. For some individuals, they may progress easily from the first to the final phases. More commonly, however, the path is not linear, and there will be moments when

---

55. Alee Robins and Amy Fiske, "Explaining the Relation Between Religiousness and Reduced Suicidal Behavior: Social Support Rather than Specific Beliefs," *Suicide and Life-Threatening Behavior* 39, no. 4 (2009): 386–395.

phases once experienced will be revisited. It is also common not to be able to move to the final phase. That is okay. Any effort made to forgive is a positive one and instrumental in the healing journey from suicidal thoughts.

Phase 1 Recognition of who or what hurt you. It is important to recognize and validate what happened to you. Journaling, confiding in a trusted person, even speaking to yourself out loud to reflect on your feelings are all helpful in finding truth in your experience.

Phase 2 Deeper Awareness in this phase occurs around what happened. You begin to feel or witness the emotions that result from the situation or event. This phase has a great deal of energy involved as potential anger is distinctly felt.

Phase 3 Personal Choice occurs when you start to recognize that the pain and anger you are carrying is hurting you, not the person who hurt you. You recognize that forgiveness has benefits for you, and even though you have not fully chosen to do so yet, your heart and spirit begin to feel more positive at the possibility of letting go in the future. A helpful practice in this phase is to identify 5 ways holding onto anger is hurting you and 5 ways it would benefit you to let it go.

Phase 4 Work Phase is when a great deal of action occurs. You may start to seek out ways to practice forgiving such as writing a letter (sent or unsent) and practicing empathy where you mentally put yourself in the shoes of the other person to understand their motives, as well as efforts to accept and reimagine the pain they caused. This work does not omit what they did, nor does it give them permission to hurt you again. Some people will speak directly to the person who hurt them about these efforts, while many do not.

Phase 5 Release happens when you no longer carry tension, anger, or resentment in your body, mind, and spirit. In this phase, you may feel motivated to let the other person know you forgive them to further release yourself from the bondage of anger. This phase may also give rise to further integration of past pain and trauma—providing further meaning for what happened. It is important to know that you can energetically reach this phase of release without speaking to or communicating with the person who hurt you. This is especially true in instances where that person has died or is not available to speak to.

A helpful practice in this phase is to identify 5 ways holding onto anger is hurting you and 5 ways it would benefit you to let it go.

Forgiveness is My Superpower

When I embrace self-love, self-forgiveness seeps into my consciousness more and more. There are times now when I come across an old photo of myself from when I was in a heightened suicidal ideation episode. I look through my eyes and into the pain, and I imagine holding that former self and whispering compassionate words to her. I offer her a clean slate filled with forgiveness for anything said, thought, or felt that pushed her to the edge of life.

In my past work, I was involved in some high-profile projects in the entertainment business, such as *Harry Potter, Fantastic Beasts, Constantine*, and *Willy Wonka and the Chocolate Factory,* as well as behind-the-scenes content and marketing for over three hundred other entertainment projects. How does this relate to forgiveness? Well, the success of those campaigns and projects hinged on our team's ability to identify, create, and maximize the superpower of that brand to the utmost. Similarly, when it comes to healing from suicidal ideation, we need to identify, tap into, and maximize every superpower we have.

When considering which superpower helps heal suffering and raises us above traumas from our past, forgiveness is undoubtedly at the forefront. It must be embraced from all directions, which can be incredibly challenging, even if it is in your nature. Forgiveness is not only for others but for yourself. We can be so hard on ourselves, but it is important to remember our minds, much like a supercomputer, will replay the narratives and experiences we regret. At times, it can seem almost as real as if we were watching a movie. So, what can we do? Again, go to forgiveness. The act of forgiving is in your control, and I would correlate it to what happens during **Phase 2: Clarity** of healing. We do not have control over many things in life, but the power to forgive is something we can always choose. The goal is not to pressure yourself to be good at it or to get to a certain level of forgiveness because even the act of trying to forgive brings the healing energy of pure love. Love heals. Love is one of the highest vibrations in the universe, which is why it is so powerful. Forgiveness can provide us relief and helps to release pain and suffering from any situation.

In thinking of my personal experience of forgiveness, I bring up my career because it was a space where I had to practice this superpower often. In my industry, I often experienced workplace bullying and harassment. This behavior was encouraged and accepted, and if I complained, I would get labeled negatively. As a traumatized person trying out new tools, much like the ones mentioned in this book, I was able to see and feel where these hurtful people's insecurities were, because we all have them. At times I would imagine them younger and how their lives might have been. Maybe they were bullied and harassed and that is why they felt it was permissible to treat me the way they did. I only have sovereignty over my actions, so remaining kind and bringing in forgiveness helped me to not only live a better-quality life but to walk the walk with integrity. Just because others are being hurtful does not mean you have to boomerang that energy back to them. That is the role of an actual healer: to take what is dark and messy and send it back with love.

I believe my success in overcoming suicidal ideation is due in large part to my ability to forgive, which has helped me cultivate deep compassion for all living things. The following energy practice can help assist you in cultivating this superpower in your own life.

Unstick Negative Energy with Forgiveness

Close your eyes and imagine a person or situation you are struggling with in front of you; if it is a person, see them sitting in a chair.

Take a moment to center your breath and ground your energy into the Earth.

Imagine a big ball of light between you that is moving any stuck energy between you.

See it shining and bringing lightness to the situation. If resistance occurs, cover it with light.

Remember we are all creative beings who hold light in this world, and we do not have to carry the heavy energy.

The Importance of Conflict Resolution

It is crucial we all learn how to manage conflict because it is the foundation of deep forgiveness work, especially if the conflict is with people you love and want to still have in your life. I try to remain open when someone hurts me and wants to talk or reconcile. Healing is important for all involved, even if it is highly challenging. Practicing conflict resolution has supported my healing from suicidal ideation. It is also healthy **not** to speak to someone who is dangerous or harmful to you. In this case, you may need a professional or a support person to guide the process. If you still wish to forgive and it is not safe to explore conflict resolution with another directly, there is much you can do from a safe distance, helping you live a better and fuller life.

Without conflict resolution, we tend to dismiss other people and situations haphazardly, which contributes to why people feel so abandoned and sad. The goal should be to come together and learn from each other, and if we must end a relationship, we can choose to leave the same way we came—in *peace*. If the world practiced more forgiveness, it would be a different place entirely. Change can start with you.

Conflict Resolution Skills that Work For Me

- Don't procrastinate and put it off too long, causing anxiety to build. Even a hard conversation can bring relief when finally communicating your feelings.

- Release expectations of what the other person may say—realizing you might never hear what you want from the other person.

- Go calmly and with an open mind as much as possible; the idea is not to agree 100 percent but that each person has an opportunity to be heard.

- Realize that if the other person is not effectively communicating, they might not have as much awareness as you do. Compassion for this reality can increase your ability to forgive, even if the conflict is unresolved.

- Engaging in meditation or being in a quiet space before the conflict can help you remain grounded during the interaction; likewise, it can help to re-engage in meditation or the practice of quiet to re-regulate yourself and reflect on what happened.

Here is an example of how I have experienced the **5 Phases of Forgiveness** in my life.

Recognition and Deepening Awareness: My best friend and I had a six-year period when we did not speak. We had both gone through unbelievable losses, and instead of coming together, we fell apart because we were both in pain and processing childhood trauma. It helped me see how our own suffering could block our perception of and compassion toward each other's experiences of suffering.

Personal Choice: Years later, we naturally started to come back together through healing and forgiveness. During this time, we both spent time on our own and together exploring our perception of the situation.

Work Phase: We didn't rush the reunion; both of us were aware rebuilding trust would be slow. With patience and time, we finally felt ready to have a completely transparent conversation about what happened to our relationship. We each apologized for our transgressions and chose to let it all go, remembering how much we treasured each other.

Release: We learned a great deal about each other and how we function in our relationship. We were able to take what we learned and establish healthy boundaries, which were necessary to forge a path forward together. Forgiving was key to mending our friendship. We continue to give each other the floor to speak our thoughts and pains as they arise, so we both feel heard and respected.◌

> *Let me disclose a particular secret about the angels of the three heavens that people have not been aware of until now because they have not understood levels. It is this, that within every angel —and within every one of us here—there is a central or highest level, or a central and highest something, where the Lord's divine life flows in first and most intimately. It is from this center that the Lord arranges the other, relatively internal aspects within us that follow in sequence according to the levels of the overall design. This central or highest level can be called the Lord's gateway to the angels or to us, his essential dwelling within us. It is this central or highest level that makes us human. —Emanuel Swedenborg,* Heaven and Hell *39*

Forgiveness Journal prompt

In reflecting on someone you wish to forgive, which phase do you currently find yourself in and what are you experiencing, feeling, and hoping for the in the situation/relationship? Use this space or write in your own journal if this is not enough room.

_____

_____

_____

_____

_____

 ## Metta Meditation

The way we think and feel toward someone can either enhance our energy and expand our ability to socially connect and feel safe, or it can retract our energy and keep us closed and guarded. Even if you do not intend to extend forgiveness to the specific person or group who hurt you, you can still practice forgiveness through the act of Metta meditation. This form of meditation is supported by theories of cognitive science[56] which explore how our thoughts impact us. This form of meditation utilizes well-wishing first for yourself, then for those you care for, then for your community, and then for a person or group you are struggling with. The practice is quite simple, yet the benefits are outstanding. Metta meditation has been found to:

- Promote self-compassion
- Decrease stress and anxiety
- Reduce physical pain
- Improve longevity and telomere health
- Enhance social connections
- Improve immune system response
- Improve sleep quality ♥

56. Jordi Manuello et al. "Mindfulness Meditation and Consciousness: An Integrative Neuroscientific Perspective," *Consciousness and Cognition* 40 (2016): 67–78, accessed October 1, 2023, https:// .sciencedirect.com/science/article/abs/pii/S1053810015300659.

A Guided Metta Practice

(3–5 minutes or as needed)

To practice this form of meditation, follow the instructions below.

- Sit or lay down in a comfortable position. Allow your eyes to close. Take a slow, deep breath in through your nose, filling your lungs and belly. Hold your breath for a moment and then slowly release it in a long, gentle exhale. Repeat this breath cycle three more times.

- Return to natural breathing. Imagine your breath traveling through your body.

- Focus on your heart.

- Begin the Metta mantra. Silently recite the phrase, directing it toward yourself first: "May I be happy. May I be safe. May I find peace."

- Slowly repeat the phrase. Acknowledge its meaning and how it makes you feel. If you get distracted, avoid judging yourself. Just return to the phrase and keep repeating it. Continue until you feel relaxed, or until you have recited the phrase at least five times to yourself.

- Next, think about your friends and family. You can think about a specific person or a group of people. Recite the phrase toward them: "May you be happy. May you be safe. May you find peace." Again, recognize the meaning and how you feel. Repeat the phrase until you experience compassionate feelings (such as a warmth in your heart or a gentle smile) or at least five times.

- Continue reciting the phrase toward others, including neighbors and acquaintances. Recognize your emotions. Repeat the phrase until you experience compassionate feelings or at least five times.

- Continue reciting the phrase toward difficult individuals or someone you want to practice forgiving. If this is too difficult, you can think of the person you want to forgive as a young child or baby. Recognize your emotions, even if they're negative. Repeat the phrase until you experience compassionate feelings.

- End by returning the phrase back toward yourself. Recognize how you feel and extend gratitude for the peace and compassion you've created. When you are ready, gently open your eyes.

Ho'oponopono (sounds like HO-PO-NO-PO-NO) Forgiveness Practice

(5–10 minutes)

This is one of my favorite practices. I do it often in my own life and encourage my clients to do the same. It is a traditional Hawaiian practice centered around reconciliation, forgiveness, and mental cleansing. It is used to put things back in the right or correct way, through adjustments, amending, and rectifying "to make good." Because conflict occurs from different people's perspectives, using intentional empathy to imagine being the other person and understanding how they may have perceived the conflict can expand the practice and enhance its benefits.

Practice

There are a few different variations online, including a larger version that the Hawaiians use, but here is the standard practice.

Sit in a comfortable position, close your eyes, and let your breath find your natural rhythm. With each exhale, let any tension drain from the body.

Address what you want to heal, clear, or forgive and any transgression you want to release including persons or groups involved—no matter who is believed to be at fault. You can say in your mind or aloud whichever of the following statements feels most powerful to you. As you say one or several, feel the emotion behind the words.

"I'm sorry."
"Please forgive me."
"Thank you."
"I love you."
"I wish you peace."

Repeat these statements over and over for as long as you can for up to 108 repetitions, which in Tibetan Buddhism is a number that connects us both to ourselves and to the world and universe around us.

At the end of the practice, take a moment to journal your reflections on what you felt before and after the practice in your body and mind:

_____

_____

_____

 KNOWING YOUR WORTH
Overcoming Doubt

When it comes to believing in healing (and the ability to forgive, as we have been exploring), there must be a sense of faith and trust in yourself. This can be especially difficult if you have ever struggled with doubt in its many forms. The fear of failing at overcoming suicidal thoughts and living a life of joy is natural, as up to this point you may have been staring at what felt like an impenetrable wall of uncertainty and self-doubt. Past experiences and a lack of confidence can both make that wall seem even higher, and the fear of relapsing to earlier phases of suicidal risk and thoughts can become incredibly profound. When considering what it means to heal, there is a lot of internal effort involved. You might not be able to see the change happening from the outside, so it is not uncommon to experience impostor syndrome in which you doubt your skills, talents, or accomplishments and are met with a persistent and internalized fear of being exposed as a fraud.

You are not a fraud. You are a work in progress.

Know that it is natural to have doubt, and it can actually serve as a motivator to continue on your healing journey if these thoughts are met with self-compassion and curiosity as opposed to fear and avoidance.

Thinking back to when we explored your parts, if your self-doubt part surfaces, get curious by trying the following.

- Meditate and sit down with this part—ask what it is needing in that moment.

- Journal as if you are writing from the part of you that doubts.

- Share your concerns with the Self Energy and seek compassion and understanding from within.

- Know that doubt is a natural part of any change.

Another thing you can consider is embracing doubt, as there are two different types:

- Stagnant Doubt: Stares at the wall and remains stuck. This type of doubt leads to inaction, insecurity, depressive symptoms, anxiety, and a pervasive lack of purpose. This type of doubt sees the wall as the whole story and either tries to walk around and avoid pain (leaving it there to deal with later) or just sits and stares at it.

- Productive Doubt: Looks at the wall and starts to explore it. This type of doubt remains curious and looks at each brick (representing old stories and false narratives) as something to remodel and even potentially deconstruct. This type of doubt is willing to say, "I don't know," and seeks to explore and ask more questions to find out what it needs. This type of doubt will engage with the wall, not denying it is there, nor engaging in bullying or self-flagellation to get through it. This type of doubt wants to learn and understand that doubt can be part of a growth mindset journey.

If you find yourself marred with stagnant doubt, try practicing curiosity using inquiry approaches with your doubtful part. Perhaps you and it are sitting at the wall together trying to coordinate a plan for healthy change. Doubt can happen anytime you try to grow, and so it is normal if you are experiencing these feelings at this point in your journey. ♡

Doubt is my Disability

If forgiveness is my superpower, doubt is my disability. It is the seesaw upon which my suicidal ideation has teetered. In the past, I would work diligently to let something go and finally feel like I was in a good place, then something would trigger me, and I felt like I was at the beginning. Doubt would hold me back from embracing my truths wholeheartedly. I believe, because I had a traumatic past and I had not done the deep healing yet, that I inherently surrounded myself with persons who probably also had trauma that was unhealed. We probably shared a commentary about how hard life was and that most people don't reach their dreams. We ruminated in negative thinking around each other without fully knowing it. So now, not only am I battling my own harsh internal wording but I am also picking up on others' self-criticism.

When you are torn inside, it is hard to see the paths that are available to you, but doubts can act as inaccurate signposts in your subconscious, stopping you from getting to the end of the road. All of us come into this world with limitless potential to learn and change any circumstance; we are the ones that stop us from moving to the places that we dream to be. Some have harder roads than others but that is what their soul is craving: a challenge to overcome, and a core lesson mastered. Whether these doubts are emerging from you, from others (such as loved ones, teachers, and colleagues), or even from social media commentary, you need to go through them with a fine-tooth comb and break them down. For example, if you have doubts because you lack information in a specific area, get the education you need to free that doubt. That is a healthy processing of doubt. If doubt causes stagnant thoughts, such as *you can't, you won't,* and *you never will,* and these thoughts elicit feelings of fear and anxiety, this is a good indicator these doubts are unhelpful. In this case, they should be filtered for truth, honored, and processed out of your thinking by any means possible.

| **If forgiveness is my superpower, doubt is my disability.** |

When I reflect on the number of times I was told I would never get published or that my authentic voice was not important enough, I look at those comments, give them a gentle bow of acknowledgment, and push them out of my energetic field. I am grateful that I did not allow them to hold me down. I kept trying and hoped that someone would see what I had to offer and give me a chance. I had an internal drive because I wanted to reach my goals so badly. I chose to stand up against doubt, look it right in the eye, and reframe it from a perceived disability into an ability. Because I have done the clearing needed in myself first, the right paths of people, projects, and opportunities have opened for me, and they will for you and your loved ones as well. I believe it with all my heart and soul.☺

Doubt Quotes to Support Your Journey

"Our doubts are traitors, and make us lose the good we oft might win, by fearing to attempt."
—William Shakespeare, *Measure for Measure*

"Our ambitions can only be limited by our doubts."
—Rajesh

"You should never, never doubt something that no one is sure of."
—Roald Dahl

"If you hear a voice within you say you cannot paint, then by all means paint and that voice will be silenced."

—Vincent Van Gogh

"The only limit to our realization of tomorrow will be our doubts of today."

—Franklin D. Roosevelt

"A hero is someone who, in spite of weakness, doubt or not always knowing the answers, goes ahead and overcomes anyway."

—Christopher Reeve

(ak) Creatively Confident

If you woke up tomorrow, and a miracle happened so that you no longer felt suicidal, what would be different? What would the first signs be that the miracle occurred?

This question is just one of many used in solution-focused brief therapy,[57] which has been found effective in supporting people to recognize the resources, as well as the reasons, to live during a crisis. An important part of the miracle question is that it encourages creative thinking. When in despair, our thoughts tend to be critical and limiting, which makes it more difficult to make lasting and meaningful change. Trying to live a life free of suicidal thoughts means no longer speaking unkindly to motivate yourself, but rather, living with

57. Johnny S. Kim, "Examining the Effectiveness of Solution-focused Brief Therapy: A Meta-Analysis," *Research on Social Work Practice* 18, no. 2 (2008): 107–116, accessed December 23, 2023, https://journals.sagepub.com/doi/abs/10.1177/1049731507307807.

a growth mindset where mistakes are an opportunity to learn and grow.

Connecting with your inner sense of confidence also means remembering what matters most to you at your core. Though it may seem simple, we receive a certain level of spiritual joy and positive biochemical feedback when we engage in hobbies or talents we enjoy. If you feel you have no passions to exercise, it can sometimes help to reflect on the people you look up to and how you may want to emulate them in your own unique way in the world. Remember, these people have their own doubts as well; it is just whether you forge ahead despite the uncertainty.

To help enliven your ability to live fully and overcome doubts about living a life free of suicidal thoughts, art is a wonderful avenue to explore. Cathy Malchiodi, author of *The Art Therapy Sourcebook*,[58] suggests that art therapy helps people work through overpowering emotions and trauma, making it a powerful resource for processing how suicidal thoughts have impacted your life. In the following exercise, we invite you to experience this power of art therapy by processing potential doubts about moving forward with a life free of suicidal ideation. ♋

A Mountain to Climb Art Directive

In the space provided (or in your own sketchbook), create an image of a mountain range to symbolize the journey you have been on and the journey yet to come. Feel free to shift the orientation of the book horizontally if you wish. On one side of the mountain, write words or create symbols for what you have overcome from your past. At the top of the mountain, create images or write words for current fears or doubts you have. On the other side, create images or write words for what you hope to overcome in the future. Also remember, there is no correct way to create these images. Whatever you feel compelled to create is exactly as it should be.

58. Cathy Malchiodi, *Art Therapy Sourcebook* (New York: McGraw Hill, 2006).

Materials: Choose any of the following—colored pencils, markers, crayons, pastels, or paints. You can also opt to create a mountain range and then make a collage using images from magazine clippings: in this case, you will need scissors and glue.

Title and date of your image: _____

_____

How did you feel while creating your image both physically and emotionally?

_____

_____

What feelings arise as you look at your image?

_____

_____

If you were inside your image, where would you be?

_____

_____

What question does your image ask of you?

_____

_____

 Have No Doubt About This: You are a Work of Art
When it comes to doubt, the most important ones to release are those centered on your personal value and uniqueness. You are irrefutably worthy, not despite but because of your distinct experiences, stories,

quirks, style choices, hobbies, and passions. Sure, we all have things we might wish to change about ourselves or our lives, but we are also amazing—perfectly imperfect pieces of art to be shared with others.

When my mind was in doubt, certain I was not worth being here, I had fallen down the rabbit hole in **Phase 3: Despair.** To process this doubt, I began to use a practice of connecting into the intelligence of my body. I would look at my hands and marvel at their functionality, or I would remember these amazing facts about my body (yours is the same):

- It houses complex digestive, muscular, integumentary, lymphatic, endocrine, nervous, skeletal, reproductive, respiratory, and urinary systems.

- It contains nearly 37.2 trillion cells.

- Its microbial biome, including bacteria and fungi, consists of 39 trillion cells.

- It takes around 22,000 breaths a day.

- Each day, its kidneys process about 200 quarts (50 gallons) of blood to filter out about two quarts of waste and water.

- It excretes about a quarter and a half (1.42 liters) of urine daily.

- It contains about 100 billion nerve cells in the brain alone.

- It is over 50 percent water.

Taking this grounding and mindful look at the marvels of your own body can open new perceptions and clear unhelpful doubts. The more you pay attention, the more you realize how much you belong here. ❧

The brain, like heaven, exists in an environment of purpose, useful purpose. Anything that flows in from the Lord embraces as its aim the salvation of the human race. This is the goal that reigns supreme in heaven and therefore in the brain as well. After all, the brain, where the human mind resides, has a goal for the body—that the body serve the soul, enabling the soul to be happy forever. —Emanuel Swedenborg, Secrets of Heaven 4054

CONCLUSION

In this chapter, we explored how overcoming suicidal ideation and potential doubts about making changes, even healthy ones, can lead to incredible growth and meaning in your life. Although painful and at times scary, overcoming and surviving this journey creates a level of compassion and empathy not all people can have for others. Because of what you have endured, you know more than most about what it is like to overcome some of the most difficult challenges in life. This makes you a warrior and a survivor.

As you not only survive but aim to thrive, remember to connect with yourself positively through creativity, seeking support from others, letting go of past pain and doubts, and choosing compassion and forgiveness for yourself and others. The more you work to let go, the more you will release the negative effects that harboring energetic anger can have on your healing journey.

The miracles of healing from suicidal thoughts and living a life where life's pains can be endured, while knowing joy is on the other side, are made possible when you choose to let go of doubt and lead with conviction. Each of these efforts brings you closer to a future centered on hope. Connect often with your sense of self-worth and your ability to see worth in others, even if they have hurt you in the past. This challenging but rewarding work makes it possible for you to move forward to the next phases of the healing journey, and creates the potential to connect with your inner gifts and reason to live. In the next chapter, we will explore ways to engage in practices designed to reconnect you to your inward source of joy, healing, and self-worth. ♥

Chapter 8: Forward

When fear is removed, hope takes its place. —Emanuel Swedenborg, Secrets of Heaven 2694

AS YOU MOVE FORWARD with new ideas and paths to follow in living a life healed from suicidal ideation, there will certainly be challenges, stressors, and barriers. *Whether* these present themselves in your life is not the question, but rather, when. Purely being human brings the potential for struggle, and that is why hope is commonly the most helpful antidote. To enhance your ability to connect with hope, this chapter contains ways to establish a hope mindset and an opportunity to use these new positive perspectives for re-envisioning your safety plan. From there, Gina will lead you in a meditation on joy to help you embody a forward momentum toward healing and growth.

ESTABLISHING A HOPE MINDSET
The Science and Power of Hope

According to nearly two thousand studies on the topic of hope,[59] the ability to think and live with this mindset has been found to be the most effective measure of well-being over a person's lifespan. When facing adversity, trauma, mental health issues, and/or suicidal thoughts, it can be difficult to imagine embodying a sense of hope. The good news, however, according to Chan Hellman, professor of social work at the University of Oklahoma and director of the Hope Research Center, is that hope is not an innate feeling, but rather, a way of thinking that can be learned.[60] This is a powerful concept when overcoming suicidal ideation because, if you can change your thoughts, you can change your sense of hope. Being hopeful is something you can practice.

Throughout this book, we have explored various ways to lead you toward the goal of living a life free of suicidal ideation. We are not merely being optimistic in our venture; rather, we understand that hope provides you with power over what happens in your life and in your future. Skills learned in this book, such as meditations, breath work, and spiritual practices, along with the insights about yourself you have gained, are necessary pathways to instill the willpower to hope for a life free of suicidal thoughts.

According to Hellman's research, there is a difference between wishing to overcome suicidal thoughts and having hope that you will overcome these thoughts. A wish is a desire for something but without ways to control, influence, or execute it. Much like a child may wish on birthday candles to become a bird, the desire is there, but the means are not.

Hope is the belief that, despite potential barriers or circumstances (such as struggling with trauma, suicidal ideation, or other limiting

---

59. Chan Hellman, "The Science and Power of Hope," *TED*, May 2021, https://www.ted.com/talks/chan_hellman_the_science_and_power_of_hope.
60. *Ibid.*

factors), tomorrow can and will be better than today because you have the power to make it so. It is a way of thinking that becomes intrinsic in how we feel when we are faced with challenges. To encourage a hope mindset, there are three important factors that must exist:

1. **A pathway** consisting of skills, methods, and means to solve problems so you can reach your desired goal or outcome. The goals explored in this book are being healed from suicidal ideation and finding moments of true joy. The pathway is the insights and practices you have learned to employ from this book.

2. **Willpower** to sustain motivation, or a sense of confidence in your ability to use these pathways to overcome obstacles. This is commonly referred to as motivation. It is important to remember, however, that you can commit to something even if you are not motivated to do it (much like waking up to an early alarm clock). However, having the willpower and motivation makes it feel more attainable.

3. **A desire for life.** The more we desire an outcome, the more likely we will remain motivated. In healing from suicidal thoughts, the desire to live can change the course of one's ability to hope. This is important and part of the mission of this book. As we mentioned in the very first chapter, we did not want to focus on how not to end your life, but rather, on reasons to live. Connecting with your desire for life can increase hope, as hope begets hope.

After experiencing suicidal thoughts for what may feel like an eternity, hope may feel hard to come by. This makes sense: suicidal thoughts are often connected to other forms of trauma and adversity, which can alter what kind of goals we set, impacting our ability and will to hope. Hellman explains[61] that when under stress, our goal-setting tends to change in these particular ways:

- Goals become short-term.
- Problem-solving skills diminish.

61. *Ibid.*

- Most of our goals focus on what we *do not* want to have happen rather than on what we do.

- Nutritional depletion becomes even more detrimental as our brains need glucose for decision-making processes.

The powerful thing in combating these effects is awareness. If you know that your circumstances or history of suicidal thoughts make it more difficult to have the willpower to reach the goals you have for healing, you can alter the way you think and how you set goals. These efforts make a big impact. For one, it may feel inauthentic to lean into optimistic goals when you are feeling suicidal or enduring stress or trauma, but in fact, you're just bypassing the barrier that normally keeps you set on avoidant goals. "I don't want to feel miserable" is an avoidant goal, as opposed to, "I want to feel joy," which is a hope-oriented goal. I often encourage my clients to practice this in session by asking them what they want as opposed to what they don't want.

Let's consider a few more ways to increase your sense of hope about recovering from suicidal thoughts and living a life of joy:

- Use your imagination. This part of your brain is connected to the compassion centers, so if you are struggling to identify creative ideas, you can overcome this by using self-compassion statements as we explored earlier in Chapter 4.

- Make sure your goals are desirable as they will be more motivating and lead to more change.

- Make sure goals are attainable. You can ensure this by using a SMART (specific, measurable, attainable, relevant, and timebound) goal. For example, this week I will journal daily to help support my healing journey from suicidal thoughts. The more you experience small successes, the more hopeful you become.

- Seek support. We gain hope from others. Finding even one person who can be hopeful or encouraging of your journey increases a hopeful mindset and makes it more likely you will know what to do (and where to turn) if you find yourself in a space of suffering or pain. ❧

At the Edge I Chose Wings to Fly

Even in my most hopeless moments of suicidal ideation, there remained this flicker of light inside of me that kept burning—my soul spark. Through tears, sorrow, and the heaviness of my suicidal ideation, I reached a dark edge where I almost fell into the abyss. That light of hope was what started to scream at me: *Get up, don't do it, walk around, call someone, draw, hug your dogs, go on a hike, shake this moment off!* I walked to that edge, and instead of falling into the abyss, I sprouted metaphorical wings and flew into my recovery, knowing there would be bumps on my way but with a renewed spirit and determination to change my future.

With time, patience, and practice, I learned that self-regulation helped me build conscious control over my thoughts and habits. I realized that I could have a life even better than before. I understood that my goal all along had been to find a meaningful path of healing. This process allowed me to fall more in love with myself than I had ever been. This light of hope shines bright and wide for all to see inside and outside of me now. Through sharing my story and supporting others, I hope to serve as a beacon of light helping others navigate through their own difficult times.

I Found the Angels through Swedenborg

During the years I struggled with suicidal ideation, I constantly sought help through spiritual and alternative healing methods. I put a horrible tattoo over the scar on my wrist. Still, it did not cover the pain, and I would later laser this tattoo off. Those marks will always be there.

I now acknowledge those battle wounds as part of my journey. I look at them differently; I am still here and thriving, able to laugh, hear music, see the stars, and fall in love. Uncovering what worked for me took some time, but my desire to live a whole life became more substantial than my desire to die.

Swedenborg entered my life around this period. I was on a lunch break from work, and in a constant state of feeling lost. I don't think I looked up at the sky for weeks. There was a small and joyous coffee shop that I used to frequent, and they had a bookstore in the center. People would also leave books behind in an area for others to browse. I was standing in line, holding my things close to my chest with my head down—which, now that I understand body language, told a story of my sorrow. I was in a period of deep suicidal contemplation. I glanced at the pile of free books and on top of the group was a picture of an angel and it seemed to be calling me as the image had this glow. I grabbed it and read the title: *Conversations with Angels* by Emanuel Swedenborg. I asked them if I could take the book home and they let me.

> **My desire to live a whole life became more substantial than my desire to die.**

I felt like the book was talking directly to me. It opened my world to angels, their work, and most important, Emanuel. I was reawakened to the fact that angels existed and, that they were all around me. I had put them out of my life as I was trying to move through the dense heaviness of my humanity here on Earth. As I read the text, I felt a lightness come back into my body and spirit. I imagined the actual dialogue between Emanuel and the angels. Him sitting there at his desk, with lamps and candles writing into the night, connecting to spirit in this way to deliver messages to us through a divine presence.

He explained how angels spiritually use thoughts and that they include thousands of nuances that earthly language cannot express. This is a knowing that I had deep inside of myself as I often struggled to find the right words to communicate the vast number of thoughts and feelings I saw permeating my mind. I started to see light and energies around me again as the darkness fell away. I wanted to know everything about angels, but more important, I was drawn to Emanuel. I thought if I could ask for communication from an angel, why not ask for communication from Emanuel? And so I did.

I would go into a deep meditative state and say, "Hello, I'd like to connect to Emanuel Swedenborg" and repeat it a few times. He answered, and I transcribed what I had heard.

When his energy arrived, it felt omnipresent, safe, and fatherly. He coughed a few times, and said, "I'm a dusty old fella for sure. I am happy that you want to share a moment with me as I am connected to you and what you will be doing in the future. I will help where I can and be with you along the way. As a writer myself, I know a few things about how this goes." He had a humorous tone and laughed while he said, "Many who knew me understand that my humor runs very deep. It makes me happy when you giggle, so please continue to do so as this is me intentionally bringing levity to what you all are up to."

Emanuel Swedenborg Messages

Through my desire to heal my suicidal ideation, I found my hidden talents not only here in the physical world but in spirit. I am a "clairvoyant cypher," which is similar to the process of the translating and downloading techniques that Emanuel exemplified. However, I do not have an IQ of 210, which makes it clear to me (at least in part) why spirit chose him to transmute these extremely complex themes. There are only three people in history, based on a research study done by Stanford University (using the Terman Standard Intelligence Test) who scored above 200—Emanuel Swedenborg, Johann Wolfgang von Goethe, and John Stuart Mill.[62]

My job is to be in service to humanity as a cypher. I communicate through written and spoken signals delivered to me to help shed light on the topics we have detailed in this book and explain them in a simplified way for many to understand.

While I was writing this, having just gone through what I would call another dark clearing of my soul's transformation, Emanuel came through in support. He let me know, "Of course, the subject matter is serious but I will not call it dark and I will not call it heavy for those words actually dampen the possibility to bring this into more light

---

62. Michael Tyman, "Swedenborg: A Genius Who Explored the Afterlife," *White Crow Books Blog.* May 2, 2011, http://whitecrowbooks.com/michaeltymn/entry/swedenborg_a_genius_who_explored_the_afterlife.

and that is your whole desire, isn't it? To bring this into the light, so I will join you and I am with you on this journey."

I sit here today as a 53-year-old soul, having found my voice and life path. I am enthralled by the mystic nature of how Emanuel Swedenborg himself in his mid-fifties, in the early 1740s, entered his spiritual phase in which he began to experience dreams and visions.[63] In this modern world, I am working through his foundation at that same age. Hope is what kept my dreams alive, as my trusted friend. I have hope that what you have read in this book will change your life for the better in deep and meaningful ways. I have hope that the world will wake up to the need for tighter communities of love and support. I have hope that every soul spark will recognize its own original beauty and liberate itself from the bondage that holds us back from living a full life. I hope everyone can celebrate their next birthday with renewed vigor, knowing that day was miraculous, because it was the day you came into the world.

Our Infinite Potential

Modern spiritualism was not introduced until 1848. Swedenborg was considered by many as the first spiritualist. The more I dug in, the more I resonated with the work of Swedenborg. I am sure you can still heal suicidal ideation without spirituality, but this was not the case for me. I needed to see, feel, and hear what I term "light language," or my own spirituality/soul vibration. As I felt disconnected from the solid, dense feeling of Earth, I went toward the energy of light to appreciate all the gifts the Earth has to offer. In doing so, I felt connection to everything! This made me feel confident that all that had happened were disguised gifts so that I may grow. For without all my stories, how could I relate to others' true suffering? How could I know and appreciate where they are and where they want to go without these experiences? I couldn't have been able to fully comprehend others' pain without my own.

63. Emanuel Swedenborg, *True Christianity*, trans. Jonathan S. Rose (West Chester, PA: Swedenborg Foundation, 2006), 687n59.

> *Our discernment cannot gain any sight unless the illusions that blind it and the distortions that becloud it are dispelled. This cannot be accomplished except by means of truths that have the inherent power to dispel distortions. —Emanuel Swedenborg,* Divine Providence *175*

I understand I am a completely different human than I was even five years ago. I cannot thank myself enough for getting through this, so I can enjoy the second half of my life, free from suicidal ideation.

I want to share another tool that I found useful: the law of "pure potentiality" based on Deepak Chopra's *Seven Spiritual Laws of Success.*[64] Pure potentiality states that, at the core of being, we are pure awareness. The realm of pure awareness is the domain of all possibilities. It underlies creativity in all its forms. Pure potentiality is pure consciousness; it is the field of all possibilities and infinite creativity. You too can embody this law of pure potentiality. It allows you to let go of things you cannot control and be willing and open to accept What Is.♡

Pure Potentiality Meditation

Bring your mind to your hopes and dreams for living a full and joyful life. You are a success in this journey of healing from suicidal ideation, simply because you are here doing this meditation.

Imagine the idea of success as an external energy, constantly being strived for—often in the form of acceptance from other people we want to impress. For this meditation, you will bring that energy back inward and understand that you as a being have all the potential you need because your potentiality is not only inside you, it is you.

Your thoughts and desires create a ripple of energy that leaves you open to all there is to experience within your stream of consciousness. As long as you are here and alive, this vibration remains alive.

---

64. Deepak Chopra, *The Seven Spiritual Laws of Success: A Practical Guide to the Fulfillment of Your Dreams* (ReadHowYouWant.com, 2009).

When we try to control our destiny and resist what is, we interfere with this vibration and the ability to remain open to all our potential. To remain open to pure potentiality, release the need to control and remain open to whatever success and healing you seek.

- Begin the active part of this mediation in a seated or lying position, take a moment to move or adjust any way you need.

- Take a slow, deep inhale, holding the breath for a brief pause. Open yourself up to the experience of this meditation.

- Follow with a slow, intentional exhale, releasing any expectations or need to control the experience.

- Repeat the openness inhale and releasing exhale at least five times.

- The use of mantra work is incredibly powerful in connecting with the vibration of potentiality as opposed to restriction and control. For this meditation, we will use the mantra: Om Bhavam Namah, or "I am absolute existence." Simply think the mantra silently or say it aloud as you breathe slowly and naturally.

- Continue this mantra for at least the next five minutes (using a timer if needed) and breathe naturally as you open yourself up to whatever happens.

- Notice any thoughts, feelings, and sensations without judgment.

- Allow the mantra to come to an end and stretch your arms overhead, gathering all your potential from around you, and bring your hands to your heart center, gathering it into your heart and soul.

Since we are by creation heavens in smallest form and therefore images of the Lord, and since heaven is made up of as many desires as there are angels, each of which is a person as to its form, it follows that the constant effort in divine providence is for each of us to become a heaven in form and therefore an image of the Lord. —Emanuel Swedenborg, Divine Providence 67

What We Think Matters

When considering what it means to live a life without suicidal thoughts, it is important to attend not only to your energy but also your thoughts and ideas around healing from suicidal thoughts. Based on Aaron Beck's cognitive behavioral therapy (CBT), the way someone perceives or thinks about a situation can become more closely connected to how they feel about it than the actual situation itself.[65] Essentially, what we think, feel, and believe has a powerful impact on our perception of reality.

Taking Beck's work a step further, we can explore how our thoughts impact our energy, not just on a subconscious or spiritual level but also in our physical body. In fact, research has shown[66] that positive thoughts not only have a boosting effect on our immune health, but they help improve blood flow to the heart and reduce chronic pain.

Interestingly, studies have also found[67] that, when speaking to growing plants in a lab with positive words, the plants grew healthier and stronger than the plants spoken to with negative words. Much like any living creature, how you speak to yourself matters! The following section explores how reframing negative thoughts from what we do not want (to suffer or experience suicidal thoughts) to what we do want (to feel joy and experience healing) positively impacts recovery from suicidal thoughts.

- Like attracts like: If you are thinking positively and feeling hopeful, your physical body and subconscious mind will respond positively. Your energetic vibration and frame of mind will likely attract more people or situations to you, mainly because you will take notice of these more positive experiences when you change your thoughts. This means if you are thinking of hurting yourself, avoiding suffering

65. "Understanding CBT," Beck Institute, accessed March 20, 2023, https://beckinstitute.org/about/understanding-cbt.
66. Neil A. Rector and Aaron T. Beck, "Cognitive Behavioral Therapy for Schizophrenia: An Empirical Review: Neil A. Rector, PhD and Aaron T. Beck, MD (2001). Reprinted from the J Nerv Ment Dis 189: 278–287," *The Journal of Nervous and Mental Disease* 200, no. 10 (2012): 832–839.
67. Daniel Chamovitz, *What a Plant Knows: A Field Guide to the Senses: Updated and Expanded Edition* (Scientific American/Farrar, Straus and Giroux, 2020).

or not feeling pain, these thoughts are experiences at a more resistant level that lead you toward what you do not want, which reduces the ability to feel hope and causes foreshortened goal setting.

- Something will always fill empty spaces: By identifying and removing cognitive distortion (unhelpful thinking styles that are often biased) about yourself and your situation, you create space for more positive things to be noticed and experienced. It is impossible to have a completely empty space in your mind, so being mindful as to whether your thoughts are helpful or not is a powerful step toward healing.

- Presence increases the ability to attract positivity: Much of our obsessive or anxious thinking happens at a time when we are not connected with our surroundings. Ensuring you are grounded allows you to focus on noticing positivity—leaving you open to making the present moment as positive as possible. If you find in this stage you are met with feeling anger, remorse, guilt, or frustration over trying to be positive when in the state of despair, you can try reframing unhelpful thoughts and emotions by looking at them as messages from parts of yourself asking for loving attention from you. Other ways to reframe unhelpful cognitions include:

  - Practicing daily gratitude
  - Visualizing your goals
  - Looking for the positives in a situation
  - Learning how to identify negative thinking
  - Using positive affirmations
  - Reframing negative events in a more positive way (often based on integration and learning)

This way of thinking can be applied to all areas of life as a means to increase the desire to live. You may also try journaling to reflect on your emotions and thoughts connected to difficult situations, so you can begin finding alternative, more helpful ways of thinking about challenges as they arise. Questions to ask yourself when reframing thoughts with a CBT lens include:

- Writing down alternative or more positive thoughts (i.e., "I am a burden to others" reframed as "My feelings matter, and safe people will listen to me").

- Practice acceptance by focusing on what is working for you and being open to what needs to be changed. Understand that even with this principle in mind, there are things and events still out of our control. The important thing here is that you are not trying to omit pain and suffering entirely, but rather, adjusting how you respond to these events when they arise.

- Use change language by remembering that what we say matters. Make statements about what you do want and why you wish to live as opposed to thinking about what you do not want.

- The power of positive focus is like riding a bike on a straight path while looking at a tree to the left and trying not to veer off and hit it. Your bike will go where you focus, and if it is not where you want it to go, you will want to refocus your attention to increase your ability to feel more positivity and joy.

Based on the principles of CBT, the following exercise encourages you to incorporate the therapeutic benefits of journaling, which can help in various ways, such as:

- Help you focus on and achieve goals
- Increase confidence
- Increase self-awareness
- Reduce stress and anxiety
- Find inspiration
- Strengthen memory
- Improve perspective
- Offer an outlet for emotional expression

When considering different forms of journaling, research suggests[68] that cognitive emotive journaling is helpful in developing awareness while finding positive aspects within a stressful event or situation. This form of journaling involves reflecting on both your thoughts and emotions about a situation as opposed to only one or the other. ♡

"What We Think Matters" Journal Prompt

The following journal prompts encourage the ability to manifest healing from suicidal thoughts. Take your time, do not edit yourself, and remain compassionate to your feelings. You can choose which prompt draws you in and do that first or do them in order.

1. What thoughts and emotions do I have about being healed from suicidal ideation?

_____

_____

_____

_____

_____

2. When considering what my worries are for my future, what are they and what thoughts and emotions do I have about them?

_____

_____

_____

_____

_____

68. James W. Pennebaker and John Frank Evans, *Expressive Writing: Words that Heal* (Enumclaw, WA: Idyll Arbor, 2014).

3. When considering what my hopes are for the future, what are they and what thoughts and emotions do I have about them?

_____

_____

_____

_____

_____

 ## CREATING A HEALING STRUCTURE

In conceptualizing my own healing, it has helped me to envision the structure of a home. A common adage says you wouldn't put the plumbing into a home without first building the foundation where it will all rest. I resonate with this visual because it suggests that there are methodical steps to rebuilding your personal healing structure, rather than an endless journey into the abyss. It helped ease my anxiety to see healing in phases, because seeing healing as one singular event can feel overwhelming. I manifest my healing structure one section at a time, before I move forward. The following questions have helped me with this process in finding what truly embodies my mission for healing and living a full life.

What is at the foundation of healing for you that helps to create a sense of safety and structure?

For me, it was about finding ways to help manage my massive anxiety, to heal familial wounds of abuse, neglect, and substance abuse, and to connect deeper to my spirituality. I also want to call in a healthy and loving partner to build my life with who understands me on my level.

How does this new foundation feel?

It feels safe and calm. I have confidence to speak up about my needs to those around me without fear that I will be abandoned or judged. I have chosen to release doubts about my future so I can enjoy my daily work and life purpose. I have also chosen to release the past events that caused self-pity and suicidal ideation. I choose to manifest healthy relationships with my family, friends, and colleagues.

Who and what can you enlist to help you?

I made a well-rounded plan that includes therapy, exercise, journaling, meditation, and other healing modalities. I have continued to engage with my spiritual education by finding more like-minded individuals who have similar interests through meetups, social media, or other outlets such as classwork at community colleges, wellness retreats, and physical trainers or teachers in a variety of sports or exercise activities.

From the answers to these questions, I can find what matters most to me and remind myself daily of what is most important to me to manifest. From there, I have created a mission statement for survival and joy, which I would like to share with you.

Gina's Mission Statement: "I Am Here in the Now"

"I am right here, and I am safe. I do not need to figure out steps seven to forty-eight. I just need to keep moving through what is in front of me. I am committing to that for the next six weeks because in those six weeks I am just living my way to the answers, not thinking my way to them because that isn't working. I am trusting. I have faith. I am safe. I am loved. I will read this every morning and night for this period of time. It is not selfish to put myself first so I can heal." ❦

Mission Statement Exercise

After reading Gina's mission statement, we would like to invite you to answer the same kind of questions to help you build your own statement:

What does your soul want you to know today?

_____

_____

_____

What is at the foundation of healing for you that helps create a sense of safety and structure?

_____

_____

_____

How does this new foundation feel?

_____

_____

_____

Who and what can you enlist to help you?

_____

_____

_____

After reading your responses, create a one- to two-sentence mission statement, much like Gina did for herself. Make sure to also put this statement somewhere visible, such as on the wallpaper of your phone, a sticky note on your mirror, or in the form of art (some even opt for body art with tattoos).

YOUR RE-ENVISIONED SAFETY PLAN
Now that you have taken the journey toward healing in the pages of this book, we invite you to revisit the safety plan you created on page 71 and add to it anything you've learned about your journey in surviving suicidal ideation. ♋

My Vows
The Safety Plan is a promise to yourself that you will follow your plan in the case that suicidal thoughts or intense struggles arise. I think of this safety plan much like a vow. Vows and rituals have become extremely important to me in my journey of overcoming suicidal ideation. Finding meaning through our promises to ourselves and others can directly affect our sense of wellbeing and willingness to commit to them. When thinking about what promises I want to make to myself and the world around me, I commit to this:

I declare this earnest promise to kindly act and live with love and compassion for myself and others as much as possible. I will continue to try and see the good, even when things feel difficult. I commit to continue to build my spiritual pathways for deeper connections. I will lean into the light and let it hold me when the hard times come. Instead of falling back into the tar pits, I will follow the intelligence of my heart and release my brain from the strain of trying to figure everything out perfectly. I will continue to practice forgiveness at even deeper levels. I will not let my voice be silenced by others who do not want to hear what I have to say, but I will still forgive them for their transgressions and pray for their healing. I will perform rituals for my ancestors and thank those who have come before and after me. I will continue to help others who are suffering by building new tools, speaking, and finding ways to connect and reach others who are seeking healing. I will continue to connect with the human collective, as I want each and every one of you to stay with us in the here and now.

STAYING FULLY ALIVE

I now have permanent tools and pathways toward hope within me to handle difficult things as they come. I am lucky to be able to see Earth through these new eyes. I am not just living, but I am thriving. I found my life purpose, which is and has always been to be "in service" to myself, those who need me, and the planet. Whichever way I leave this Earth, I know it will not be by my own hands, and I welcome my destined ending whenever that comes to be. Until then, I want to hear music, climb the hills, dive into the oceans, observe wildlife, meet people and listen their stories. I want to put my arms around fellow humans and pour as much love into their hearts as I can. I have released the chains of my self-imposed prison because I now have all the keys to set myself free as I have become the Liberated Healer. 🫀

I am Joy Meditation

(10 minutes)

This final meditation is performed standing to allow energy to flow freely, bringing you back fully into your power. If you are unable to stand, choose any position that feels comfortable. Set the environment with calming natural lights or candles.

- Stand barefoot to better connect with the Earth, with your feet hips-distance apart.

- Keep your eyes open, as this helps you remain present with your mind and body connection.

- Stand tall and pull your shoulder blades back toward each other, opening your heart space.

- Pull your hips or buttocks back to help align yourself by resetting the natural S curve in the spine and support your lower back.

- Keep your knees slightly bent (not locked).

- Imagine there is a white string moving from the base of your spine up through the center of your body and out the top of your head to the clouds, as well as downward into the Earth below.

- Take three deep breaths into the nose, expanding your diaphragm, and exhale the air out of your mouth.

- Return to natural breathing.

- Let your arms rest at your sides with your palms faced outward, open to receive.

- Tuck your chin to your chest and roll your head toward the left three times and then to the right three times.

- Relax your jaw and close your eyes.

- Imagine a giant golden sun on the back of your shoulders growing larger and larger as it fills with liquid joy. When the sun is large enough, allow it to burst and cover your entire being.

- Say out loud, "I am joy." Repeat this several times with conviction and repeat the golden sun cycle at least three or more times.

- If you are able, raise your arms overhead and stretch them to the sky. Fold your fingers in on each other, forming a steeple, and let your head fall back gently, giving way to a slight back bend.

- Return your head to neutral and slowly fold yourself toward your toes, reaching for the ground. Imagine any weight you are carrying in life falling off your shoulders and out the crown of your head into the Earth.

- Roll yourself up slowly, bringing your head up last.

- Allow yourself to smile if it feels good and say again, "I am joy."

None but those who have experienced a state of peace can appreciate the nature of the peaceful tranquillity that the outer self enjoys when there is an end to struggle, or to the disquiet of burning desires and misconceptions. That state is so joyful that it surpasses all our notions of joy. It is not simply an end to our struggles but a vibrancy welling up from deep-seated peace, affecting our outer being beyond the capacity of words to describe it. —Emanuel Swedenborg, Secrets of Heaven 92

 ## CONCLUSION

As we close the journey of discovering what you have to live for and how to find it, remember that external factors, such as material success, perfection, acceptance, or the pursuit of happiness, are impermanent achievements. Even if we could erase trauma and suffering completely, there can still be a void. That is why it is imperative you continue to go inward and connect with your spiritual, physical, and mental parts, as well as the "soul spark" that Gina has explored throughout this book. By using this spark and other insights learned along the way, you now have the tools to manifest and attract what and who you want and need by remaining open to the pure potentiality of your consciousness and all that life has to offer.

We encourage you to become actively engaged in this book for the rest of your life. Mark it up, draw on it, dog-ear it, place bookmarks and notes directly into it. It's a working, breathing document of the journey you have chosen, the journey to live. Come back to the pages that most resonated at times when life becomes difficult or suffering resurfaces—all of this is part of your healing journey. Remember that the **5 Phases of Suicidal Ideation,** the **5 Phases of Healing from Suicidality,** and the **5 Phases of Forgiveness** can flash before you all within one day's time. What matters is your new level of awareness that passing through these phases is also impermanent, as no feeling is final. As we have seen on the journey through the forest of suicidal ideation, seeing the horizon of healing, finding pathways, and resting in your wholeness and worth, there is much to feel hopeful for. We, the authors, would love to hear about your story of survival and healing and welcome your input and insights about how this book affected you. There is a great mystery in what is to come, much to learn, and many souls beyond your own who will benefit from your knowledge and experience of healing from suicidal ideation.

Epilogue

It makes not the slightest difference whether some of us are far apart on the planet, even if the distance is many thousands of miles; we can still be together in the same community. If we exercise kindness in our lives, we are in an angelic community.
—Emanuel Swedenborg, Secrets of Heaven 1277

 ## DR. KELLEY'S LETTER TO YOU

First and foremost, I want to tell you how glad I am that you are here. Experiencing the things that lead the human mind and heart toward suicidal thoughts and then surviving that through whatever means possible is a testament to your extreme strength. I am aware that in the deepest and darkest moments it might feel like no one is out there and no one's listening, but I assure you we are. We are waiting in the wings, eager for the moment you open your heart and let us see inside. I understand there are going to be people who do not know how to handle your heart, but I assure you, if you remain open to pure potentiality and keep looking, you will find the right people who can. Sometimes, this means cutting off certain relationships and finding a trusted therapist; other times, this means finding fellow survivors of suicidal ideation and leaning on one another. If you feel like you have not found that person, please keep looking. I assure you they are there. When I think of the clients who have trusted me with their own heart, I am eternally grateful every day they choose life. No matter how little hope they come into my office with, I continue to assure them that I will indefinitely provide my hope for them. The messages about hope in this book really stood out to me. The more I learned about the different facets of what can impact suicidal ideation, the more I realized how universal these themes and experiences are. How human they are. Hope is at the core of any change we try to make, any risk we try to take, and any emotional hill we aim to climb.

In my personal life, my work, and my writing, I am constantly seeking empowerment messages, much like how Gina is drawn toward spiritual practices. I seek to learn more about the way the human brain interacts with empowerment through experiences, relationships, and energetic shifts in the environment. If changing our messaging internally from *wishing* to *hoping* can make as dramatic a difference as I have learned it can, then that message itself provides me hope. I extend this hope to you, with my most sincere and driven desire that you find something within these pages that resonates for you. Although, I am realistic, and I know not all of it necessarily will. Please lean into whatever that practice, theory, or guiding message is and run empathically with it toward healing.

When I think of my interactions with suicide before writing this book, I recall an era of prevention. As a therapist and as a survivor of generational trauma, I admit I still carried a seed of fear within my heart for the people experiencing these thoughts. What I have learned from Gina, the research, the open conversations with others, the personal stories, and other lessons along the way is that we need not fear these thoughts and feelings; rather, we need to be present for them with open arms. We need to be students, as well as teachers, in constant conversation and compassionate dialogue about this topic. It needs to be on our lips every chance we have and every time it comes across our path.

To Gina, my coauthor and courageous survivor, I am so grateful for your patience and grace in pulling me out of the halls of my research mind and encouraging me to connect with what we cannot see and touch. Your courage in not only sharing your authentic story but in being vulnerable with me during this process has changed me forever. I am renewed in the knowledge that my creative mind is right next to my analytical one, and they can sing and dance together.

To the Swedenborg Foundation, I am honored that you created a space for us to share this message with all of those who are meant to hear it. I deeply anticipate our continued partnership and all of the things I will learn and experience that I would not have, had our paths not crossed.

Finally, to my husband and family, thank you for your support and patience as I navigated not only the time spent on writing this book but the emotional experiences I endured as I cultivated a greater understanding of the topic. When I write, I immerse myself in a topic much like a method actor. As a highly sensitive person, writing about a facet of the human experience becomes a felt sense and a vicariously lived experience during my writing process. Sometimes this can lead to strong emotions and responses to what I am learning, and with a topic as important as this, that was certainly the case. I love you for believing in me and patiently waiting for me as I tap the last few strokes on the keyboard and close my laptop with pride—until the next project comes along, of course. ✒

GINA'S LETTER TO YOU

It's in nature for all living things to evolve and have but one goal: survival. Humans are unique because we decide what, when, where, and how deeply we grow and change. Given our opportunities, would other mammals make the same decisions as us? When you wake up to the fact that every twenty-four hours is loaded with potential and lean into the upward spiral of positive emotions more often, the dark thoughts, feelings, and stories start to lose power over you. In the space where they used to live, there is room to call in and manifest the life you envision for yourself, which you wholeheartedly deserve. Not only will you most likely get it, but you will be able to hold it through chaos and conflict with love, kindness, laughter, and gratitude. You will want to expand your knowledge and share it with all who will lend you an ear. As soon as you picked up this book, my spirit connected to you, and my prayers and guides (which include Emanuel Swedenborg) have been holding space for you to heal, as that has been my life's work since making my shift to the last and final phase of healing, **Phase 5: Confidence.** The secret blessing is that I've also received healing from you, as it's a two-way street because there is always a give and take in energy exchange. No one person is more important than another. I invited the unknown and leaned into this journey with you. I too have changed since the birth of this written expression. Thank you for seeking new ways to help yourself and others. Each person who makes this journey helps elevate the world around them. Let's remain curious about what is on the other side of healing together. If you are not at this place, please know we are holding space for you to heal. I truly understand. Eventually, we are confident you can get to a place where you say, "Not one more day will be filled with suicidal ideation." I dedicate this co-creation with spirit and Emanuel Swedenborg to each of you. Thank you for your trust and belief.

I also would like to thank all of those who have helped me in my journey. I request forgiveness from those who I have hurt and I would like to offer my forgiveness to anyone who has hurt me. Thank you for pushing me to my edge of the mountain so I could see the vast vistas and recognize their beauty, so I could sprout wings and float back down to Earth gracefully.

I'd like to recognize my partnership with Dr. Amelia Kelley, who, through her patience and brilliance, has truly made this experience one of the highlights of my life. This was a guided and divine union—you are forever in my heart. Thank you for your undeterred dedication to helping those souls who need someone like you to lift them. May the wind be ever at your back, and may you always be guided by the angels of hope and deep knowingness.

To the Swedenborg Foundation team and Emanuel Swedenborg: This union is a blessing beyond words. I've felt your presence every step of the way and am delighted to go on this adventure with you. Thank you for your hard work and desire to raise people up through learning and your incredible collection of work and for believing in projects like this.

To my mother, Patricia Palmer. I am proud to be your child.

To my paternal siblings, from our father Gino "Robert" Chevalier, thank you for being in my life and helping with my parental wounds.

To Sicily Sunshine, who helped push the dark sediment out with your prayers to help me complete this expression.

To Gloria Ann Manu Kanemura Bentley (Hula dancer) for giving me my first book on hot yoga.

To Diane Ladd (actress and friend) for giving me my first book on Kabbalah and healing.

To all the healing friends, practitioners, shamans, teachers, students, and clients who shared space with me so we could practice our magical gifts of light.

In loving memory of my dear friend, Kari King, who passed away from an unfair illness while I was working on this book. I felt your gentle spirit sit with me to find the poetic words when I needed them.♥

Resource Guide

Crisis Lifelines

911 for any emergency in the United States of America and for immediate medical assistance for ambulance transport to a hospital. If you are having suicidal thoughts, it might be better to look at the options below with people trained in listening to your specific needs. You don't have to be suicidal to use these lines; you can if you just need an empathetic ear or to ask what you can do to help someone else.

988 and/or **1-800-SUICIDE** (1-800-784-2433): The National Hopeline Network will connect you with a counselor based on your area code; push 1 for Veterans or text 838255; push 2 for LGBTQA+; and for TTY users, use your preferred relay service or dial 711. Chat at 988lifeline.org.

Canada Kids Help 1-800-668-6868 and **Parents Hotline** 1-888-603-9100: bilingual and anonymous phone counseling and referral service for children.

CDC National HIV and AIDS Hotline: 1-800-232-4636.

Center for Elderly Suicide Prevention (CESP) Friendship Line: 1-800-971-0016 (ioaging.org). 24/7 hotline for seniors, family members, caregivers, and advocates.

Childhelp National Child Abuse Hotline: Call or text 1-800-422-4453. For issues related to child abuse, Childhelp connects you with professional counselors to help in a crisis and to provide information on how to get help. They offer phone support in 170 languages, or you can chat online with a counselor.

Cop 2 Cop: 1-866-267-2267 (cop2coponline.org). 24/7 assistance from law enforcement offices.

Covenant House Nineline: 1-800-999-9999 (covenanthouse.org). Crisis intervention, referral, and information services to troubled youth and their families.

Crisis Text Line: Text Hello to USA/741741, UK/85258, Canada/686868. Use phone, WhatsApp, or Facebook. Crisis Text Line fields messages about suicidal thoughts, abuse, sexual assault, depression, anxiety, bullying, and more. What makes it unique is that it's entirely text-based, which makes it easy for anyone who doesn't feel comfortable or safe talking on the phone to use it.

Focus Adolescent Services: 1-877-362-8287 (focus.com).

Girls and Boys Town National Hotline: 1-800-448 3000 in English/Spanish (girlsandboystown.org/). Serving children and families in a variety of ways.

LGBTA+ Senior Hotline: 1-888-234-7243.

LGBTQA+ National Hotline: 1-888-843-4564.

National Domestic Violence Hotline: Text START to 88788 or call 1-800-799-7233.

National Hopeline Network: 1-800-784-2433.

National Resource Center for Suicide Prevention and Aftercare: 1-770-541-1114.

National Sexual Assault Hotline: 1-800-656-4673.

National Suicide Prevention Lifeline: 1-800-273-8255.

Not My Kid, Inc.: 1-602-652-0163.

RAINN: 1-800-656-4673. The Rape, Abuse & Incest National Network's hotline is for anyone who has experienced sexual abuse or assault. When you call its main hotline, you'll be connected with someone at a local organization in your area who can provide live support and direct you to additional resources. RAINN also offers live chat on its website.

Substance Abuse and Mental Health Services Administration National Helpline: 1-800-662-4357.

The Trevor Project: 1-866-488-7386 or text START to 678678. LG-BTQIA+ kids and teens can reach out to the Trevor Project for support during a crisis, if they are feeling suicidal, or need a safe space to talk about any issue. You can also chat via their website or by texting START to 678678.

Trans Lifeline: 1-877-565-8860. The Trans Lifeline provides support specifically for transgender and questioning callers. They provide support during a crisis and can also offer guidance to anyone who is questioning their gender and needs support.

Veterans Suicide Crisis: Text Hello to 838255.

YouthLine: Text teen2teen to 839863 or call 1-877-968-8491. Youth-Line provides a safe space for children and adults aged 11 to 21 to talk through any issues they may be facing, including eating disorders, relationship or family concerns, bullying, sexual identity, depression, self-harm, anxiety, and thoughts of suicide.

Suicide Prevention and Mental Health Organizations

American Association of Suicidality (AAS) suicidality.org

American Foundation for Suicide Prevention (AFSP) afsp.org

American Psychiatric Association Practice Guidelines for the Assessment and Treatment of Patients with Suicide Behaviors psych.org

Center for Mental Health Services Knowledge Exchange Network (KEN) mentalhealth.org

Children's Safety Network (CSN) childrenssafetynetwork.org

Injury Control Research Center for Suicide Prevention (ICRCS): suicideprevention-icrc-s.org

Jed Foundation jedfoundation.org

Kristin Brooks Hope Center changingthepresent.org

National Alliance for the Mentally Ill nami.org

National Association for People of Color Against Suicide nopcas.com

National Institute of Mental Health nimh.nih.gov

National Center for Post-Traumatic Stress Disorder—Veterans Assistance ptsd.va.gov

Organization for Attempters and Survivors of Suicide oassis.org

Suicide Awareness Voices of Education save.org

Suicide Prevention Resource Center sprc.org

Trevor Project thetrevorproject.org

Yellow Ribbon Suicide Prevention yellowribbon.org

Twelve-Step Organizations

Adult Children of Alcoholics adultchildren.org

Alcoholics Anonymous alcoholics-anonymous.org

Al-Anon/Alateen al-anon.org

Co-Dependents Anonymous codependents.org

Narcotics Anonymous na.org

Overeaters Anonymous overeatersanonyous.org

Suicidal Ideation Anonymous Under development by Gina Cavalier

Suicide Anonymous suicideanonymous.net

Survivors of Incest Anonymous siawso.org

Book Recommendations

Ace Your Life—Unleash Your Best Self and Live the Life You Want by Michelle P. Maidenberg Ph.D., MPH, LCSW-R

Anxiously Attached: Becoming More Secure in Life and Love by Jessica Baum

Better Than Before: What I Learned About Making and Breaking Habits—to Sleep More, Quit Sugar, Procrastinate Less, and Generally Build a Happier Life by Gretchen Rubin

Complex PTSD: From Surviving to Thriving by Pete Walker

Complete Book of Meditation—A Comprehensive Guide to Effective Techniques for Calming Your Mind and Spirit by Shai Tubali

Conversations with the Z's—Awaken Your Multidimensional Soul by Lee Harris

Healing Self-Injury, A Compassionate Guide For Parents and Other Loved Ones by Janis Whitlock Phd and Elizabeth Lloyd-Richardson Phd

Many Lives, Many Masters—The True Story of a Prominent Psychiatrist, His Young Patient, and the Past-Life Therapy That Changed Both Their Lives by Brian Weiss, M.D.

No Bad Parts—Healing Trauma and Restoring Wholeness with the Internal Family Systems Model by Richard Schwartz

No Will Set You Free—Learn to Say No, Set Boundaries, Stop People Pleasing, and Live a Fuller Life by Michael J. Tougias

Parts Work: An Illustrated Guide to Your Inner Life by Thomas Holmes

Recovering You—Soul Care and Mindful Movement for Overcoming Addiction by Steven Washington

Self-Compassion: The Proven Power of Being Kind to Yourself by Kristin Neff

Speak: Find Your Voice, Trust Your Gut, and Get from Where You Are to Where You Want to Be by Tunde Oyeneyin

The Body Keeps the Score: Brain, Mind, and Body in the Healing of Trauma by Bessel van der Kolk

The Gaslighting Effect: How to Spot and Survive the Hidden Manipulation Others Use to Control Your Life by Dr. Robin Stern

The Highly Sensitive Person's Guide to Dealing with Toxic People: How to Reclaim Your Power from Narcissists and Other Manipulators by Shahida Arabi

The Journey from Abandonment to Healing—Surviving through and Recovering From the 5 Phases that Accompany the Loss of Love by Susan Anderson

Unlock the Power of Your Chakras—An Immersive Experience through Exercises, Yoga Sets and Meditations by Masuda Mohamadi

Whole Brain Living—the Anatomy of Choice and the Four Characters that Drive our Life by Jill Bolte Taylor, Ph.D.

Apps to Help

Most apps are free or there is a free trial period to see if you like them before having to purchase a membership.

Aura aurahealth.io

Calm calm.com

Daylio Journal daylio.net

Feeling Good app.feelinggood.com

Headspace headspace.com

Insight Timer insighttimer.com

Moodflow Mood Tracker moodflow.co

Operation Reach Out A suicide prevention app for veterans and military families, available on all app stores.

PTSD Coach mobile.va.gov/app/ptsd-coach

RIA Health riahealth.com

Smiling Mind smilingmind.com.au

Stay Alive stayalive.app

SunnySide.co sunnyside.co

Bibliography

American Psychiatric Association. Diagnostic and Statistical Manual of Mental Disorders: DSM-5. Washington, D.C.: American Psychiatric Association, 2013.

American Psychiatric Association, DSM-5 Task Force. (2013). "Substance-Related and Addictive Disorders." In *Diagnostic and statistical manual of mental disorders: DSM-5™ (5th ed.).* American Psychiatric Publishing, Inc. https://doi.org/10.1176/appi. books.9780890425596.

Aron, Elaine N. *The Highly Sensitive Person: How to Thrive When the World Overwhelms You.* New York: Kensington Publishing Corp., 2013.

Bach, Donna, Gary Groesbeck, Peta Stapleton, Rebecca Sims, Katharina Blickheuser, and Dawson Church. "Clinical EFT (Emotional Freedom Techniques) Improves Multiple Physiological Markers of Health." *Journal of Evidence-based Integrative Medicine* 24 (2019): 2515690X18823691.

Baldoni, Justin. *Man Enough: Undefining My Masculinity.* HarperCollins, 2021.

Bjelland, Julie. "Are Highly Sensitive People More Susceptible to Suicide? Survey Results Including Recommended Resources." January 20, 2023. https://www.juliebjelland.com/hsp-blog/are-highly-sensitive-people-more-susceptible-to-suicide-survey-results-including-recommended-resources.

Bongiorno, Peter. "A Cold Splash–Hydrotherapy for Depression and Anxiety." *Psychology Today,* July 6, 2014. https://www.psychologytoday.com/us/blog/inner-source/201407/cold-splash-hydrotherapy-depression-and-anxiety.

Bowen, Sarah, Neha Chawla, Joel Grow, and G. Alan Marlatt. *Mindfulness-based Relapse Prevention for Addictive Behaviors.* New York: Guilford Publications, 2011.

Boyd, Jenna E., Ruth A. Lanius, and Margaret C. McKinnon. "Mindfulness-based Treatments for Posttraumatic Stress Disorder: A Review of the Treatment Literature and Neurobiological Evidence." Journal of Psychiatry and Neuroscience 43, no. 1 (2018): 7–25.

Burroughs, Josephine L. "Marsilio Ficino, Platonic Theology." *Journal of the History of Ideas* (1944): 227–242.

Cannon, Dolores. *Between Death & Life: Conversations with a Spirit.* Ozark Mountain Publishing, 1993.

Cecco, Leyland. "Are Canadians being Driven to Assisted Suicide by Poverty or Healthcare Crisis?" The Guardian. May 11, 2022.

Chamovitz, Daniel. *What a Plant Knows: A Field Guide to the Senses: Updated and Expanded Edition.* Scientific American/Farrar, Straus and Giroux, 2020.

Chopra, Deepak. *The Seven Spiritual Laws of Success: A Practical Guide to the Fulfillment of Your Dreams.* ReadHowYouWant.com, 2009.

Dennison, Adam. "The History of Cold Water Immersion: A Timeline." *Cold Plunge Facts.* 2023. https://coldplungefacts.com/cold-water-immersion-history.

Doss, Richard. "Trained Not to Cry: The Challenge of Being a Soldier." YouTube Video. July 21, 2023. https://youtube.com/watch?v=WkCq6BWFBAM.

Dunne, Claire. *Carl Jung: Wounded Healer of the Soul.* Watkins Media Limited, 2015.

Favaro, Avis. "Woman with Chemical Sensitivities Chose Medically-Assisted Death After Failed Bid to Get Better Housing." *CTV News.* Updated August 24, 2022. https://www.ctvnews.ca/health/woman-with-chemical-sensitivities-chose-medically-assisted-death-after-failed-bid-to-get-better-housing-1.5860579.

Ferguson, Monika, Kate Rhodes, Mark Loughhead, Heather McIntyre, and Nicholas Procter. "The Effectiveness of the Safety Planning Intervention for Adults Experiencing Suicide-related Distress: A Systematic Review." *Archives of Suicide Research* 26, no. 3 (2022): 1022–1045. https://www.tandfonline.com/doi/abs/10.1080/13811118.2021.1915217.

Frankl, Viktor E. *Man's Search for Meaning.* 1959. Reprint, Boston: Beacon Press, 2006.

Hallford, David J. "Most People Don't Disclose Their Suicidal Thoughts." *Psychology Today.* April 22, 2023. https://www.psychologytoday.com/us/blog/our-wonderful-messy-minds/202304/we-dont-talk-about-ending-our-lives.

Harris, Russ. ACT *Made Simple: An Easy-to-Read Primer on Acceptance and Commitment Therapy.* New Harbinger Publications, 2019.

Hellman, Chan. "The Science and Power of Hope." *TED.* May 2021. https://www.ted.com/talks/chan_hellman_the_science_and_power_of_hope.

Hillman, James. *Suicide and the Soul.* (1973).

Hof, Wim, and Koen De Jong. *The Way of the Iceman: How the Wim Hof Method Creates Radiant, Long-term Health—Using the Science and Secrets of Breath Control, Cold-training and Commitment.* Dragon Door Publications, 2017.

Holmes, Thomas R., Lauri Holmes, Sharon Eckstein, and Jane Eckstein. *Parts Work: An Illustrated Guide to Your Inner Life.* Kalamazoo: Winged Heart Press, 2007.

How Common is Trauma. The National Council for Mental Wellbeing. Accessed April 9, 2024. https://.thenationalcouncil.org/wp-content/uploads/2022/08/Trauma-infographic.pdf.

Joshi, Chetan Arvind. *An Empirical Validation of Viktor Frankl's Logotherapeutic Model.* University of Missouri-Kansas City, 2009.

Kelley, Amelia. *Gaslighting Recovery for Women: the Complete Guide to Recognizing Manipulation and Achieving Freedom from Emotional Abuse.* New York: Random House, 2023.

Kelley, Amelia. "Signs of a Toxic Relationship: Are You in a Trauma Bond?" Amelia Kelley, January 18, 2023. https://www.ameliakelley.com/quiz/signs-of-a-toxic-relationship-are-you-in-a-trauma-bond/.

Kleiman, Evan M., and Richard T. Liu. "Social Support as a Protective Factor in Suicide: Findings from Two Nationally Representative Samples." *Journal of Affective Disorders* 150, no. 2 (2013): 540–545. Accessed August 22, 2023. https://doi.org/10.1016%2Fj.jad.2013.01.033.

Kim, Johnny S. "Examining the Effectiveness of Solution-focused Brief Therapy: A Meta-Analysis." *Research on Social Work Practice* 18, no. 2 (2008): 107–116. Accessed December 23, 2023. https://journals.sagepub.com/doi/abs/10.1177/1049731507307807.

Lazar, Sara W., Catherine E. Kerr, Rachel H. Wasserman, Jeremy R. Gray, Douglas N. Greve, Michael T. Treadway, Metta McGarvey et al. "Meditation Experience Is Associated with Increased Cortical Thickness." *Neuroreport* 16, no. 17 (2005): 1893–1897. Accessed September 1, 2023. https://.ncbi.nlm.nih.gov/pmc/articles/PMC1361002/.

Linehan, Marsha. *DBT Skills Training Manual*. New York: Guilford Publications, 2014.

Malchiodi, Cathy. *Art Therapy Sourcebook*. New York: McGraw Hill, 2006.

Mayo Clinic Staff. "Tests and Procedures: Psychotherapy." *Mayo Clinic*. April 11, 2023. https://www.mayoclinic.org/tests-procedures/psychotherapy/about/pac-20384616.

McAllister, Kimberly. "Making and Breaking Connections in the Brain." UCDavis Center for Neuroscience. University of California, Davis. Accessed August 21, 2023. https://neuroscience.ucdavis.edu/news/making-and-breaking-connections-brain.

Menakem, Resmaa. *My Grandmother's Hands: Racialized Trauma and the Pathway to Mending Our Hearts and Bodies*. Las Vegas, NV: Central Recovery Press, 2017.

Mooney, Brenda. "Despite Expanded Efforts by VA, Veteran Suicides Rose Slightly in Recent Report." *U.S. Medicine*. December 6, 2023. https://www.usmedicine.com/block/despite-expanded-efforts-by-va-veteran-suicides-rose-slightly-in-recent-report/.

Moore, Thomas. *Care of the Soul, Twenty-fifth Anniversary Ed: A Guide for Cultivating Depth and Sacredness in Everyday Life*. Harper Perennial, New York, 2016.

Neff, Kristin. *Fierce Self-Compassion: How Women Can Harness Kindness to Speak Up, Claim Their Power, and Thrive*. London: Penguin Books Limited, 2021.

Manuello, Jordi, Ugo Vercelli, Andrea Nani, Tommaso Costa, and Franco Cauda. "Mindfulness Meditation and Consciousness: An Integrative Neuroscientific Perspective." *Consciousness and Cognition* 40 (2016): 67–78. Accessed October 1, 2023. https://.sciencedirect.com/science/article/abs/pii/S1053810015300659.

Pennebaker, James W., and John Frank Evans. *Expressive Writing: Words that Heal*. Enumclaw, WA: Idyll Arbor, 2014.

Philips, Dave, "A Secret War, Strange New Wounds, and Silence from the Pentagon." *New York Times*. Updated March 15, 2024. https://www.nytimes.com/2023/11/05/us/us-army-marines-artillery-isis-pentagon.html.

Porges, Stephen W. *The Pocket Guide to Polyvagal Theory: The Transformative Power of Feeling Safe*. First edition. New York: W. W Norton & Company, 2017.

"Prevention Strategies: A Comprehensive Public Health Approach to Suicide Prevention Can Decrease Risk." The Centers for Disease Control. Accessed April 9, 2024. https://.cdc.gov/suicide/prevention/index.html.

Sharma, Pravesh. "8 Common Myths About Suicide." *Mayo Clinic Health System*, December 20, 2021. https://.mayoclinichealthsystem.org/hometown-health/speaking-of-health/8-common-myths-about-suicide.

Substance Abuse and Mental Health Services Administration (SAMHSA). *Treatment for Suicidal Ideation, Self-harm, and Suicide Attempts Among Youth*. SAMHSA Publication No. PEP20-06-01-002, Rockville, MD: National Mental Health and Substance Use Policy Laboratory, Substance Abuse and Mental Health Services Administration, 2020.

Rector, Neil A., and Aaron T. Beck. "Cognitive Behavioral Therapy for Schizophrenia: An Empirical Review: Neil A. Rector, PhD and Aaron T. Beck, MD (2001). Reprinted from the J Nerv Ment Dis 189: 278–287." *The Journal of Nervous and Mental Disease* 200, no. 10 (2012): 832–839.

Restrepo, Sandra, dir. *The Call to Courage*. 2019; Los Gatos, CA: https://www.netflix.com/title/81010166/

Rizk, Mina M., Sarah Herzog, Sanjana Dugad, and Barbara Stanley. "Suicide Risk and Addiction: The Impact of Alcohol and Opioid Use Disorders." *Current Addiction Reports* 8 (2021): 194–207.

Robins, Alee, and Amy Fiske. "Explaining the Relation Between Religiousness and Reduced Suicidal Behavior: Social Support Rather Than Specific Beliefs." *Suicide and Life-Threatening Behavior* 39, no. 4 (2009): 386–395.

Schnarr, Eleanor Mariakali, "Door of my Heart: Comparative Internal Breathing in Yogananda and Swedenborg," June 2023. https://.spiritualquesters.org/wp-content/uploads/2023/06/Door-of-my-Heart-ODB-1.pdf.

Schreiber, Flora Rheta. *Sybil: The Classic True Story of a Woman Possessed by Sixteen Separate Personalities.* Regnery Publishing, 1973.

Schwartz, Richard C., and Martha Sweezy. *Internal Family Systems Therapy.* Second edition. New York London: The Guilford Press, 2020.

Seo, Eun Hyun, Hae-Jung Yang, Seung-Gon Kim, and Hyung-Jun Yoon. "Ego-resiliency Moderates the Risk of Depression and Social Anxiety Symptoms on Suicidal Ideation in Medical Students." *Annals of General Psychiatry* 21, no. 1 (2022): 19. https://pubmed.ncbi.nlm.nih.gov/35717375/.

Shapiro, Francine. *Getting Past Your Past: Take Control of Your Life with Self-help Techniques from EMDR Therapy.* New York, NY: Rodale Press, 2013.

"Suicide and Self-Harm Injury," Centers for Disease Control and Prevention. Accessed April 9, 2024. https://.cdc.gov/nchs/fastats/suicide.htm.

Swedenborg, Emanuel. *Divine Love and Wisdom.* Translated by George F. Dole. The Portable New Century Edition. West Chester, PA: Swedenborg Foundation, 2010.

———. *Divine Providence.* Translated by George F. Dole. The Portable New Century Edition. West Chester, PA: Swedenborg Foundation, 2010.

———. *Heaven and Hell.* Translated by George F. Dole. The Portable New Century Edition. West Chester, PA: Swedenborg Foundation, 2010.

———. *Secrets of Heaven.* Translated by Lisa Hyatt Cooper. Vol. 1. 15 vols. The Portable New Century Edition. West Chester, PA: Swedenborg Foundation, 2013.

———. *Secrets of Heaven.* Translated by Lisa Hyatt Cooper. Vol. 2. 15 vols. The Portable New Century Edition. West Chester, PA: Swedenborg Foundation, 2012.

———. *Secrets of Heaven.* Translated by Lisa Hyatt Cooper. Vol. 3. 15 vols. The Portable New Century Edition. West Chester, PA: Swedenborg Foundation, 2022.

———. *Secrets of Heaven.* Translated by Lisa Hyatt Cooper. Vol. 4. 15 vols. The Portable New Century Edition. West Chester, PA: Swedenborg Foundation, 2010.

———. *Secrets of Heaven.* Translated by Lisa Hyatt Cooper. Vol. 5. 15 vols. The Portable New Century Edition. West Chester, PA: Swedenborg Foundation, 2023.

———. Secrets of Heaven. Translated by Lisa Hyatt Cooper. Vol. 7. 15 vols. The Portable New Century Edition. Royersford, PA: Swedenborg Foundation, 2023.

———. *Secrets of Heaven.* Translated by Lisa Hyatt Cooper. Vol. 8. 15 vols. The Portable New Century Edition. Royersford, PA: Swedenborg Foundation (forthcoming).

———. *Secrets of Heaven.* Translated by Lisa Hyatt Cooper. Vol. 9. 15 vols. The Portable New Century Edition. Royersford, PA: Swedenborg Foundation (forthcoming).

———. *Survey; Soul-Body Interaction.* Translated by Jonathan S. Rose and George F. Dole. The Portable New Century Edition. West Chester, Pennsylvania: Swedenborg Foundation, 2022.

———. *True Christianity.* Translated by Jonathan S. Rose. Vol. 1. 2 vols. The Portable New Century Edition. West Chester, PA: Swedenborg Foundation, 2008.

———. *True Christianity.* Translated by Jonathan S. Rose. Vol 2. 2 vols. The Portable New Century Edition. West Chester, PA: Swedenborg Foundation, 2011.

———. *True Christianity.* Translated by Jonathan S. Rose. Vol. 1. 2 vols. West Chester, PA: Swedenborg Foundation, 2006.

"The Four Horsemen: Stonewalling." The Gottman Institute. Accessed March 30, 2024. https://www.gottman.com/blog/the-four-horsemen-stonewalling/.

"The Link Between PTSD and Suicide." Psych Central. Accessed April 9, 2024. https://psych-central.com/ptsd/ptsd-suicide.

The ManKind Initiative. "Real Men Do Cry." YouTube video, August 17, 2016. https://www.youtube.com/watch?v=PbjBc9CipBg.

Tyman, Michael. "Swedenborg: A Genius Who Explored the Afterlife." *White Crow Books Blog.* May 2, 2011. http://whitecrowbooks.com/michaeltymn/entry/swedenborg_a_genius_who_explored_the_afterlife.

"Understanding CBT." Beck Institute. Accessed March 20, 2023. https://beckinstitute.org/about/understanding-cbt.

Whitlock, Janis, and Elizabeth Lloyd-Richardson. *Healing Self-injury: A Compassionate Guide for Parents and Other Loved Ones.* Oxford University Press, 2019.

World Health Organization. "Suicide Prevention." Accessed April 9, 2024. https://www.who.int/health-topics/suicide.

About the Swedenborg Foundation

THIS BOOK WAS PRODUCED by the Swedenborg Foundation, an independent nonprofit organization dedicated to making Emanuel Swedenborg's thought more widely known and freely available to all.

Connect with us at www.swedenborg.com to read Swedenborg's writings for free and learn more about our latest offerings.

Join millions of others exploring Swedenborg's teachings at youtube.com/offthelefteye.

Deepen your exploration and connect with others by becoming a Community Member.
Members receive 30% off all books in our bookstore among a variety of other benefits.